P9-AFS-570

ALSO BY MARY KAY BLAKELY

American Mom
Wake Me When It's Over

Red, White, and Oh So Blue

A Memoir of a Political Depression

◆

Mary Kay Blakely

A LISA DREW BOOK

Scribner

A LISA DREW BOOK/SCRIBNER
1230 Avenue of the Americas
New York, NY 10020

Copyright © 1996 by Mary Kay Blakely
All rights reserved, including the right of reproduction in
whole or in part in any form.

SCRIBNER and design are trademarks of Simon & Schuster Inc.
A LISA DREW BOOK is a trademark of Simon & Schuster Inc.

Set in Adobe Janson Text
Designed by Brooke Zimmer

Manufactured in the United States of America

1 3 5 7 9 10 8 6 4 2

Library of Congress Cataloging-in-Publication Data

Blakely, Mary Kay, date
Red, white, and oh so blue: a memoir of a political
depression/Mary Kay Blakely.
p.   cm.
"A Lisa Drew book"
1. United States—Politics and government—1993–
—Philosophy. 2. Blakely, Mary Kay. I. Title.
E885.B53   1996   96–18549
320.973—dc20   CIP

ISBN 0-684-82450-7

To Phyllis,
lover of the long shot,
who talked me out of a coma and into the next dream.

Contents

PROLOGUE

The Bystander Blues

I'M GOING HOME next week. I'm not cured, exactly—there is no cure for my condition, certainly no quick or permanent one. But the staff at the Americana coffeehouse down the road was encouraged when I got through the entire newspaper this morning without asking for more Kleenex. Shirley, the unflappable matron who runs the pancake ward here in Conway, Michigan, doesn't mind stirring up a lively political debate between the vacationing golfers and local mechanics, but weeping at the counter is discouraged. It's too contagious, and everyone's immune system is shot after the verbal artillery from the campaigns this year. The general gloom over the state of the union has grown so heavy among the Americana regulars, even Shirley wasn't risking questions any more provocative than "Sausage or bacon?"

I was in such critical condition when I arrived from New York four months ago, so mute with disbelief over the meanness and mendacity professed in the name of "we Americans," that Shirley's simple question about cholesterol alternatives was an intellectual challenge. Since bleeding hearts were already goners in the current political scene, I told her just to give me whatever would put me out of my misery most swiftly.

Sausage on the side did not bring deliverance, as it turned out. My clock radio rudely informed me each morning that I was still very much alive, still facing gruesome facts and unmet deadlines and vague responsibilities. I made the transition from bed to desk as gingerly as possible, usually pausing in the doorway of my rented cabin, coffee cup in hand, to scan the horizon. If I was lucky, I would find the tall crane standing again at the end of my pier, elegant and still, a dignified gray silhouette backlit magnificently against the predawn orange sky. Undisturbed by noisy honks from the more cacophonous genera waking up in the neighboring wetlands, the crane aroused in me an intense yearning for such purity of species, such singular focus on the duties of the day.

I would take the long route to the Americana those mornings, walk along the shore of Crooked Lake, and find more reasons for gratitude as the sun came up and the loons swam by. While I know it's naive to romanticize nature, that even poets will acknowledge its cruelties and destruction, a solitary crane sighted on my pier could still make me believe the world is more beautiful than not. It's only after I would cross the road and approach the vending machines, where I obtained reports of what my species had been up to for the last twenty-four hours, that I'd lose faith in this vision.

I have a chronic psychological condition that author Kurt Vonnegut identified twenty years ago as "a political disease," afflicting people whose minds lack the essential "damping apparatus" that prevents us from "being swamped by the unbelievability of life as it really is." The symptoms are exactly the reverse of the problems many Beltway insiders have with "the vision thing," as our former president described his inability to see the effects certain

policies might have on people who didn't live in Kennebunkport. Unlike the happy campers on Capitol Hill, people
suffering political depression can see and imagine infinite
consequences for every human action. Something disturbing and violent erupts in Ruby Ridge or Oklahoma City, say,
and we think we can trace its genesis to a war in a jungle
halfway around the world, involving millions of conscripted
citizens and paid for with unimaginable amounts of tax
money. If the damping apparatus does not kick on, people
suffering political depression could even start thinking this
tragedy in Oklahoma City might have something to do with
us, with the daily acts of violence in our own cities, the rage
and futility we are feeling in our own neighborhoods. Politics becomes excruciatingly personal to us.

Without this essential filtering equipment, people who
feel a sense of emergency about all the guns and greed and
ignorance and racism rupturing our country can't get
through the daily news without experiencing "a kind of psychic hemophilia," as writer Joan Frank describes it. She
recalls the immense difficulty a friend had trying to read the
morning paper while she was recovering from a nervous
breakdown: "She had 'no boundaries,'" Frank writes, "her
whole being would flow into, or fuse with, the ghastly news
reports. Her ability to individuate from the chaotic stream
was temporarily lost." My own symptoms had become so
pronounced by the time I left New York last spring, I was
stuffing my pockets with packets of tissue before leaving my
apartment, just in case I needed to sandbag another flood at
the newsstand.

A single headline—"Three U.S. Marines Abduct and
Rape 12-Year-Old Girl in Okinawa"—could overwhelm me
with an angry rush of startled, anguished, haunting questions about what, why, how this grievous sentence could be
true. I would listen to the Japanese official later that morning on National Public Radio trying to explain his country's

outrage: "You must understand . . . our people don't do this to children. This is not a violent culture." And though I know that last assertion is not entirely true, I'd hear him to mean: "We are not like you." Most Okinawa islanders have no context in which to fit this stupefying crime. They do not get rape like we get it here, every forty-five seconds according to the New York *Daily News;* their citizens hardly even pack guns, let alone blow each other up with high explosives. I would then read the follow-up story the next day, thinking I was now prepared to face what it is we Americans must understand about our culture, what we have to change to stop this violence; instead, I would learn the major worry of the military brass was whether "the unfortunate incident" in Okinawa would lead to more *base closings.*

Because writers are never entirely off duty even as readers, I naturally notice the use of words, how the twelve-year-old girl and her family are "disappeared" in a four-column story about how many bases, the number of troops, the length of stay, and the damage our withdrawal could do to the local economy. Our military spokesmen are so gifted in public relations, so rehearsed in the methods of secrecy and obfuscation, they can make the casualties of whole wars disappear into faceless facts about "collateral damage" and amiable regrets about "friendly fire." At first I might argue with a military and a media who pass this doctored reality along—There are *friendly* bullets? These are *unfortunate* accidents?—but then inevitably . . . I was back to the blues, the feeling of vast futility that we may never address the changes that could someday relieve us of these headlines, may never remedy the myriad daily habits that result in explosions over Japan, one kind or another.

Any story about rape can now aggravate the swollen part of my brain where those facts are stored. Thirteen years ago, I had been assigned by *Ms.* magazine to write a think piece about the pool-table rape in New Bedford, Massachusetts, when the nation was stunned to learn that the nine bystanders in Big Dan's Bar had not only failed to stop the crime but cheered it on. Americans were still capable of being appalled back then. Before the Trial of the Century turned murder charges into a spectator sport, it was unseemly to cheer for men who battered women. I spent several months that year trying to put together all the parts of the sum—all the television shows, movie plots, magazine photos, advertising come-ons, religious prejudices, coaching practices, and rape jokes, all the little bits of daily life that could accrue to a crime of this size.

I was working at home in Michigan then, raising two young sons, and the devastating facts I was amassing in my office started leaking into my family room. I would stand in the doorway those Saturday mornings as the boys, still in pajamas and shaking off sleep, watched their favorite cartoons. They stared blankly into the blue glow of the TV screen, not laughing, not even smiling, just taking in another part of the bystander training program as Brutus pounded Popeye and dragged Olive Oyl off by the hair, kicking and screaming . . . always the same plot, week after week, in friendly animation.

The dam between my professional and personal life was under water by the time I read a study by professors Neil Malamuth of UCLA and Edward Donnerstein of the University of Wisconsin: 66 percent of their college subjects— normal men, regular guys—had what Malamuth called a "conquest mentality" toward women. Only one third said there was no possibility they could be sexually violent. It made me *crazy* to think my sweet, funny sons had a 66 percent chance of becoming bystanders to rape someday, if they became part of the present culture. Lose my sons or change the country . . . what choice did I have?

Even if motherhood had ever been a strictly milk-and-cookies job, it certainly wasn't by 1983. My generation, obliged to act on what we'd learned during the social-justice movements of the sixties and seventies, had to rethink every step of the socialization process, uproot every weed of prejudice in the way we taught children to talk, argue, express frustration, get what they needed, use what they've got. Unable to contain my think piece to a reasoned assembly of data, I wrote it from both sides of my journalist/mother brain, grabbing readers by the lapels and pulling them into my panic.

I apologized to my editor, Ellen Sweet, when I finally turned in the manuscript two weeks late and four times over the assigned length. Familiar with my apologies and usually a steady navigator through my verbal tempests, Ellen was having a bout of psychic hemophilia herself over the news from New Bedford. The mother of a little girl, she was especially alarmed that the old argument "she asked for it" was steadily gaining credence through media coverage of the trial. How could this be? Hadn't we already spent an entire decade deconstructing "she asked for it?" Hadn't we marched by the hundreds of thousands to Take Back the Night—shouted into loudspeakers that "No means No!" whatever the hour, the place, the previous expectations? Hadn't Ted Koppel heard *any*thing from that noisy decade when he asked a guest on *Nightline* whether the New Bedford residents interviewed earlier in the broadcast were correct in their judgment that the woman who'd run screaming from Big Dan's that night, battered and naked and terrified to insensibility, had probably *asked for it?*

Ellen went to the wall for more space while I wrestled my passions down for the count; then readers from all over the country poured their angst into letters, describing the watercooler discussions and public speak-outs that prompted action in their own cities. For several months in 1983, women from coast to coast became splendidly "strident and hysterical"—as those who take the news personally invariably sound to those who take it more professionally, sitting down, objectively evaluating it as possible material for televised games of verbal badinage.

Those of us who see the news in living color right before our eyes, imprinted on the future of loved ones, naturally get on the nerves of the political professionals who don't really mean it when they shout at each other on CNN's *Crossfire*, a kind of media friendly fire with blanks. Everyone will be back next week for another round, like the weekend warriors who play army and shoot each other with plastic guns and paint pellets. Outside the studio where the headlines are lived, it's much harder to take this gaming perspective. When people with my political sensitivities observe thoughtless contributions to the violence in our neighborhoods, we hold everyone personally responsible. Even nice guys like Popeye and Ted.

"Outsiders are often surprised, and sometimes offended, to discover that people in Washington don't take politics very seriously," *Crossfire* commentator Michael Kinsley wrote in a reflective essay in the *New Yorker*. "The premise that politics is 'only politics'—a thing apart from real life and genuine personal relationships—liberates politics itself to be that much more cynical, nasty and dishonest."

Kinsley, who is obviously still capable of shock, was deeply offended when a publicist representing Christian Coalition president Ralph Reed asked him for a promotional blurb. The only thing he and Reed have in common, Kinsley said, is that they "appeared together several times on *Crossfire*, where we have essentially called each other the Antichrist. Yet in 'Washington' it was not unreasonable to suppose that our calling each other the Antichrist is a bond we share, and that I might be happy to engage in an act of mutual hype between consenting adults."

Politics has become so gaming, sports slogans routinely substitute thoughtful discourse on the most serious social issues: "Three strikes and you're out!" is how most citizens remember Clinton's crime bill, though legal analysts were nearly unanimous that such a universal policy was economically and judicially insupportable. "Go, Juice!" appeared on makeshift signs when football fans lined overhead bridges during the celebrated Bronco chase. And when the propaganda for Operation Desert Storm reached its heights before the United States incinerated the homes of Baghdad civilians, my neighborhood grocery store was selling posters of the flag bearing the slogan "U.S.A. Kicks Butt" or "These Colors Don't Run." It's hard to imagine a civilization where crime, death, even war itself could be more fun.

As the talking heads on television have turned news into entertainment and the critical faculties of viewers have shrunk to sound-bite–sized thoughts, politics has become so unserious that Mary Matalin and James Carville could actually overlook their differences and get married. How could the major strategist for the Clinton campaign fall in love with the major strategist for the Bush campaign after each had hurled mighty insults at the other, flinging such contemptuous verbal grenades into their opposing camps that only the buildings were left standing?

In Kinsley's critique of *All's Fair*, their coauthored memoir explaining how this marriage of Arsenic and Old Lace works in real life, he remarked that it "wallows in cuteness and contains not a drop of insight into the question of how you can love someone whose values you purport to despise." Their political differences would no doubt cause serious marital strife if politics were about values, related to actual life, but politics today is all about spin. Since character is less important than image and substance is secondary to slogans, Matalin and Carville have much more in common as political celebrities than their differences as each other's Antichrist. The James and Mary Show could play for years if they speak public relations at the breakfast table with the same facility they broadcast it nationally. Their twenty-fifth anniversary cards to each other might say: "I love you . . . who are you, anyway?"

Since my work as a cultural reporter requires me to keep up with current events, often tracking several interlocking issues, it had been my habit to read the newspaper with a highlighter in hand. I'd then go back and clip whatever I'd highlighted, and place it in one of my desktop files for later reference. Toward the end there, my daily *New York Times* looked like it had been hit with a Day-Glo spray gun. The whole nation, the whole world, was alarming to me.

I didn't know where to file anything anymore. Unwieldy stacks of newsprint with electrifying headlines piled up on my desk, awaiting some organizing principle. Where to send the marines: Gang Violence? Military Morale? Child Abuse? Family Values? Foreign Relations? Do I copy the story, cross-file it everywhere? Or do I stuff it into the bulging accordion file of toxic facts about our times, where stories about sex and violence and religion and radio shows and militias and media spin were all somehow related to each other? I naturally recognized the obvious signs of burnout, an occupational hazard in my line of work. I was rapidly becoming what my friend Norma calls "a crispy critter."

Author Blanche Cook was having so much trouble maintaining her equilibrium last spring as she traversed the slopes between the morning newspaper and her research on World War II, she was losing her innocence about American politics in two decades at the same time. After dinner one evening, still swamped several hours after reading the Sunday *Times* and filing away her clips, she sighed heavily and said, apropos of nothing, "It's so hard."

"What?" her friend Claire asked, raising her eyebrows at this vague despair from her normally articulate companion. "*What's* so hard?"

Blanche shrugged. "The twentieth century."

* * *

Jane O'Reilly was so concerned about the soul-sickness that was traveling like a flu among her writer friends, she organized a monthly self-help group. She ran it like a twelve-step program, beginning each meeting with a round of introductions: "My name is Mary Kay, and I am a writer. I am addicted to words, and the compulsion to try to alter reality with them . . ." Invite a bunch of blue women over for Chinese takeout, pass a bottle of wine around, and two hours later, we can't help ourselves, we're telling hilarious depression stories. One member called us "the monthlies," since every twenty-eight days or so we could count on a laugh. We'd feel better immediately, get back to work, then start to feel the strain again before the next cycle, when some of us became borderline homicidal. Cartoonist Libby Reid said these evenings were like "therapy for women who notice too much," and launched a strip under that title in the New York *Daily News* a few months before the Sunday cartoons were downsized. Libby's now out in Portland, making jewelry. Jane herself pulled up stakes and moved to a small town in Vermont, where she became a justice of the peace. But they were our only success stories. The rest of us are still writing, and even for Libby and Jane it's one day at a time.

It's hardly surprising that writers suffer a high incidence of political depression. We are the canaries in the coal mines of civilization, the first to keel over from toxic facts that could eventually level us all. Virginia Woolf believed the hypersensitivity among our species was necessary, producing secretions vital to our work: "The shock-receiving capacity is what makes me a writer," she wrote in her essay "Moments of Being." "A shock is at once in my case followed by the desire to explain it. I feel that I have had a blow," but not "simply a blow from an enemy hidden behind the cotton wool of daily life; it is or will become a revelation of some order." When the pain of shocking truths became unbearable, she found only one reliable cure: "I make it real by putting it into words . . . I make it whole," she prescribed, for "this wholeness means that it has lost its power to hurt me."

It would be a violation of species to inoculate against this sensitivity, though writers routinely succumb to the hope that keeling over would be less painful on alcohol or drugs. Maybe it is, but garbled warnings from the semiconscious are rarely intelligible—no one can figure out exactly where the pain is, what we could or should be doing about it. If canaries are to be of any use to the rest of the population, especially as the pain threshold starts dropping all around us, I'm afraid it's our job to remain acute until the coroner arrives.

For me, the process of writing was like a gallstone operation, removing hard chunks of material irritating a tender interior. When I finished surgery on a story, the patient had to be stitched up neatly and prepared for visitors, preferably in good spirits—but on critical deadlines, cogent would do. Before my damping apparatus jammed completely last spring, I had been working on another think piece about welfare reform. My assignment was to restore human faces and stories to the numbing statistics and slogans, to analyze the new legislative proposals "in a way that won't make everybody's eyes glaze over," as my editor directed. Since it was impossible to consider welfare policies apart from what I already knew about unemployment, wage discrimination, health care, day care, teen pregnancy, post-divorce poverty, racism, and sexism, not to mention twenty years of motherhood, I was having focus problems myself. Trying to assemble a 3,500-word puzzle without benefit of the big picture, without any borders, I should have realized this project was doomed from the start.

Nevertheless, I went into the field every day to collect intelligence from the front, starting on the Upper West Side where poor people lived on the sidewalk right outside my building. But I could have started anywhere in Manhattan. It was impossible to walk through the downtown area of any American city today without encountering lifeless bodies laid out on every block, the parched bottom layer of the trickle-down economy. The ubiquitous population known as "the street people" now includes our mentally ill, unemployed, illiterate, and impoverished citizens as well as crack addicts and petty criminals, the collateral damage from our domestic War on Drugs. Whatever their route to the streets, all across America today "one saw *a people*; a poor nation living on the leftovers of a rich one," British journalist Jonathan Raban observed in *Hunting Mr. Heartbreak*. "They were anthropologically distinct, with their skin eruptions, their wasted figures, poor hair and bony faces."

This reality apparently doesn't look so bad if you take it in through numbers and indexes in the *Wall Street Journal*, where investors declare a "good economy" if profits are up. There is scant coverage on the business pages, and rarely any photos, of people going down. Mothers and children are so invisible in the national news, investors probably don't even know we are out here, laboring in the same economy. Business columnists have uniformly regarded the collapse of communism as "the triumph of capitalism." Triumph? From the front window of my apartment, capitalism without compassion looked a lot like Calcutta.

Without adequate emotional armor, it's hazardous to visit this Other America, talk to its peoples, which is why most Manhattan residents don't. Daily witnesses to the ever more cruel chasm between the haves and have-nots, the mostly middle-class pedestrians running errands on Broadway aim their eyes on the horizon and don't break stride between the grocery store and home—not because they don't care but because they care enormously. You have to go blind through Manhattan today or you'd never get to work. The boundaries for civilian observers in the War on Poverty have become so constricting, you can't walk through any park, stand in any movie line, wait at any traffic light without first killing all human responses: Don't look, don't answer, don't think, don't—especially don't—let yourself feel anything. There are enough reasons on just one block to feel lousy all day.

Sustaining the zombie state is hard for most people, and I saw my neighbors losing it all the time. They would reach into their pockets and find some spare change, often releasing a few words with the coins . . . maybe the name of a shelter or soup kitchen, maybe a heartfelt "God bless you." People holding hands with small children can almost never remain zombies. They have to walk slowly, pause to look at everything, answer "Why?" every two minutes, think hard all the way to the video store . . . where hopefully all the comedy shows haven't already been rented for the day. How do you teach children it's important to care about people at school and at home, but okay to slaughter their feelings for the nation in between?

My daily trips into the field were taking a toll. I've never successfully established any distance from street people—I keep thinking they're my relatives. I still scan their faces for signs of my brother Frank, even though I know it's irrational since I delivered the eulogy at his funeral more than a decade ago. I'm more or less resigned to my role as an easy mark for panhandlers, especially those with obvious symptoms of mental illness. Frank's madness used to terrify me, as it did him, and I spent years looking into his wild eyes on psychiatric wards, trying to make eye contact, trying to stare fear down by knowing it. If you make eye contact with panhandlers, know their stories, the buck in your pocket is already in their hands. I think of these tiny contributions as payments against my huge debt to all the strangers who were kind to Frank.

We lost him periodically, between hospitals and mental institutions, a jail cell and home—those scary times when this frail, brilliant, desperately ill young man was "out there" somewhere, totally dependent on the compassion of strangers. Walking through my neighborhood, I still make sidewalk diagnoses of manic depression, autism, schizophrenia, paranoia . . . all being treated on the streets since political reformers of the sixties stopped "warehousing" the mentally ill. Few voters back then understood that the loathsome warehouses were the last stop for the most helpless, or that the alternative to inept and underfunded hospitals would be no care at all.

A theater of the absurd, America's sidewalks reflect the insanity of a national health care policy that now jails the mentally ill before treating them. Before one Michigan mother could establish that her severely schizophrenic son was "dangerous to himself or others"—a requirement for admission to the only available state hospital—she had to apply for a restraining order and have him arrested for trespassing.

"I cried when the cops came," she said. "There is no dignity in this system, for him or for me."

It's even harder for voters to understand welfare reform today, especially since the canaries in our national press corps—who must have been on drugs the whole time our actor president was starring in "The Voodoo Economist Goes to Washington"—are still reporting political spin as if it were fact. On my way into the field every day, I would stop at the newsstand to buy the latest installments of disinformation. It's always dispiriting to read what Washington insiders have to say about my relatives and neighbors, but I needed to be fluent in the ways media handlers pureed the language with phrases like "personal responsibility" and "compassion fatigue," turning them upside down and inside out until dizzy readers exited the pages with an unsteady grip on reality.

Just as the reporters covering the New Bedford trial from defense attorney's headquarters eventually convinced a significant number of readers that the woman in Big Dan's Bar had probably "asked for it," many readers today now think that phrase explains why welfare recipients don't deserve help or compassion. If voters are told enough times that poverty is not so much a money problem as a character problem, they might actually be persuaded that hardworking, responsible middle-class taxpayers were being squeezed dry by greedy welfare moms lazing around the inner city, having more children to make extra *money*.

"My clients are poor but not stupid," said my longtime friend Joan Uebelhoer, a county welfare director in Indiana, the first state to pass the Personal Responsibility Act. Welfare mothers were profiting a whopping fifty-nine dollars per month before the "ten-month rule" eliminated benefits for new babies—saving the taxpayers less than they spent on the governor's postage stamps for a week. "Calculated by the hour, my mothers were getting rich at about seventeen cents an hour," Joan said. Less, if they had to get up in the middle of the night. The monetary compensation for raising children was so far below the minimum wage it didn't even cast a shadow. Promising to "restore dignity to the poor," character reformers in Indiana promised to "Put welfare mothers to work!"—which should have sounded weird to anyone familiar with all the toilet training, face washing, tooth brushing, grocery shopping, errand running, bedtime reading, and nocturnal worrying it takes to keep a little Hoosier alive and thriving.

Every mother works, often round the clock, yet opinion

polls showed the majority of us Americans are now convinced that poor children can raise themselves. "The 'ille-
gitimate' child of the past is the 'unqualified' child today,"
Joan said wearily, then sighed. "I thought we'd already established that you don't punish children for having the wrong
birthday." The savings to taxpayers were negligible, but the
consequences for the neediest mothers and children would
be devastating. "There is so much female loathing in this
legislation," Joan said, ". . . and people don't even hear it."

With "she asked for it" already firmly implanted in the
American psyche, the hate campaign against the poor had a
ready constituency. Living where I was and knowing what I
did, it gave me vertigo to read what I was supposed to think
if I wanted to count myself among "normal Americans." I
watched with horror as the trajectory of middle-class rage
was twisted and bent downward, now aimed at our most
undefended citizens. Aware of the war drums beating in
Washington, building bystander enthusiasm for the coming
invasion of the Other America, I didn't know where to aim
my little 3,500-word round of ammunition. A rhinoceros
was charging, and I had a pub dart. I would pack up my
notes at the end of the day and walk back through the killing
fields right outside my door, feeling the same sense of constant emergency that a doctor would have after researching
cancer all day, then stopping on the way home to unwind in
the intensive care unit.

My aptitude for detachment, when it's working, derives
largely from an episode at St. Vincent's Hospital some ten
years ago, where I spent my first nine days in New York in a
coma. This may have been the best introduction to living
in Manhattan, since so many people here seem to be in a
persistent vegetative state. Technically, the diagnosis was
"ketone-acidosis and adult respiratory distress syndrome"—

in lay terms, a diabetic in deep trouble, drowning in fluids produced by her own immune system. But I eventually came to regard my physical breakdown as a grand mal seizure of despair.

The pulmonary infections that finally knocked me out in 1984 were preceded by several megaton explosions in my personal life: my ten-year marriage to a man I still loved had ended that year; the strains of post-divorce poverty and working motherhood coincided with the sudden appearance of ominous gray shadows on my X rays; and most critically, I was still wrestling with an unresolved grief after Frank, my beloved madman brother, had permanently quit the scene the year before. The ensuing blues that winter numbed the emotional assaults from all directions—including the warning signs of serious illness. I never saw the coma coming. It arrived painlessly in the middle of the night on March 23, 1984, the final mushroom cloud after a long period of escalating psychological strife. I was never actively suicidal. I was simply willing to let the germs take me.

I have by now spent so much time wrestling with depression I no longer think of it as a disability. The blues are as natural—as awesome actually—in the range of human responses as joy or happiness. I don't even consider them something to be gotten rid of, to be conquered. Unlike clinical depressions that can be treated with prescriptions, a psychological depression takes skill and endurance, riding the bull through the pen, struggling against despair and cynicism and hopelessness. My blue periods are those intervals of blank space before the whole comes together, when my imagination is stumped for answers. I have some shocking facts, a lot of painful questions, but meaning still eludes me.

When an unwelcome new truth starts to penetrate a fiercely defended consciousness, the blues are an emotional

anesthesia for the wrenching pain as another layer of innocence is stripped back, another shocking truth becomes
real: The happy marriage is over . . . He really is dead . . .
You definitely need help. I know the coming revelation,
whatever it is, will eventually be valuable—it will change the
way I think, no doubt the way I'll have to live. But when it's
still buried in the blue haze, advancing but not here, it feels
only frightening.

"There's nothing struggled against so hard as coming-
to," Saul Bellow's depressed hero says in *Henderson the Rain
King*. "It is too bad, but suffering is about the only reliable
burster of the spirit's sleep." While each of my previous
"moments of being"—as Woolf described those painful
stretches when consciousness starts to expand—yielded
some little nugget of truth, that nine-day crater produced
what Aldous Huxley called "the individual's metanoia, or
change of mind," when the whole landscape shifts "out of
the temporal into the eternal order." For nine days I floated
through what Huxley identified as "that everlastingly possible psychological condition"—known more commonly,
among its seekers, as peace.

My previous understanding of "the peace that passeth
all understanding" was that there was an incomprehensible
serenity out there somewhere beyond reason, and therefore
beyond human capability. I interpreted that biblical passage
to mean: Give up on peace . . . mere mortals can't grasp it.
"Passeth" had thrown me. I thought it meant you had to
wire around reason to get to peace, turn off all rational
thinking. In the long recovery months after my coma, I discovered peace came *with* understanding: it was the byprod-
uct of constant thinking and striving.

And peace would go the moment I lost this picture.
Maintaining it after I returned to reality meant holding the
tension between the world I dreamed of and the one I had,
for it is that tension between Huxley's temporal and eternal

where human life is lived. While we are stuck with mortal minds and fragile bodies, limited to only baby steps toward greater knowledge on this one finite planet, everything we do here matters. It is accepting responsibility for how much we matter that finally distinguishes us from the cranes, which are merely beautiful. Our species, we Americans, can also be meaningful.

Soldiers have their war stories, writers have their breakdowns. No matter how old I become or how many dramas I eventually survive, I'll probably never stop thinking about that life-altering sleep. While the struggle of coming to and amending thirty-seven years of previous thinking was certainly hard, as the suffering Henderson reported, it's even harder to weave your altered self back into the same family, same profession, same world. After I was reborn, my overnight conversion took the greater part of the next decade. There were often frictions with those who didn't approve of all the changes I was making after my personal metanoia altered the way I worked, raised my sons, talked with friends, dealt with colleagues. Fortunately, my worry reflex had been completely fried in the great circuit crash of 1984. My close brush with death established a new bottom line for my anxiety level: If nobody dies, it's not an emergency.

I didn't have to worry as much about being disapproved of, because I'd made an astonishing discovery immediately after I woke up. While I'd been sleeping, my family and friends held the equivalent of a nine-day wake, remembering all the things we'd said and done, lived through and laughed about. They thought about all the hurts, too, and all the words that would have been said if only they'd known the clock was ticking. And then, when medical reports suggested the entity I had been was gone for good, they all did this: *Everyone forgave me.*

Imagine, waking up into an atmosphere of uncondi-
tional love at age thirty-seven, after you've already offended
almost everyone who matters to you. A near death, as opposed
to the thing itself, provided me and my family with the rare
opportunity to live the amnesty we exchanged. However
briefly it lasted—once I was up and running again, so was
the list of complaints—I actually experienced the dream
every waking adult can only have in the shower: All anyone
wanted from me that year was to remain upright, conscious,
and breathing. Everything else was background music.

It's unfortunate that the threat of death is the most common route to understanding and tolerance, because it generally occurs when we've run out of time to practice them.
For the Christian mothers of sons with AIDS, the general
fathers of Agent Orange victims, the nuclear physicists of
irradiated populations, death invariably brings home
lessons that prejudices or ambitions distract us from learning sooner. When Republican strategist Lee Atwater was
dying of an inoperable brain tumor, he invited *Life* magazine to record the profound metanoia of his final days. He
publicly apologized for the ruthless politics and manipula-
tive lies that had destroyed opponents' careers and sank the
hearts of citizens everywhere into the depths of cynicism.
Forgiving his enemies, he said he hoped they could forgive
him as well.

After his funeral, some unrecoverable cynics suggested
that Atwater's final bedside press conference was the ulti-
mate public-relations coup—like Richard Nixon, he managed to die admired after a life of political crimes. Given my
own close brush with death, I had an easier time believing
his transformation authentic. When I read *Life*'s coverage of
Atwater's death, it occurred to me that civilization would
advance much more rapidly if a diagnosis of terminal illness
were required for anyone aspiring to national office. A sense
of imminent death on Capital Hill could replace the current

lust for power, money, weapons, sex—all the earthly obses-
sions you can't take with you—with an urgent need for
greater understanding, the only environment peace can
inhabit.

I became something of a talk-show missionary after I published a memoir about my coma, entreating stressed-out,
frazzled women all over the country not to wait for a
tragedy to initiate the changes we desperately needed. I
realized that for the same amount of time and money it cost
to have a nine-day coma, I could have spent a year walking
the beaches of Key West and come to many of the same
conclusions . . . if only I had given myself permission to take
some recovery time. I made a promise the year I was
"reborn": Do something before you keel over next time.

While the profound sense of alienation I began to feel
again last spring was immediately familiar, the cure for my
cultural depression did not depend on changes in my personal life but in the political world I now occupied. My
identity crisis was not as an individual but as one of "we
Americans"—I couldn't find my place in the body politic
anymore. I battled an overwhelming sense of invisibility
every time I read opinion polls, even though I knew they
gave a skewed reflection of the country. Consciously or not,
respondents tend to choose what they perceive to be the
"right answer," especially when being "different" in America has become more and more risky. And while pollsters
might control their representative samples for gender, religion, age, voting history, and income, they rarely represent
the residents in the Other America, or any of the Ameri-
cans-to-be without green cards who are watching our kids
and bagging our groceries, contributing to our economy
and exercising our politicians, unacknowledged though
they are.

In the funhouse mirrors of political spin, I couldn't find

my political definition. I was in the margins of "we Americans" no matter which bully was speaking from the pulpit: I couldn't identify with Pat Buchanan's homophobic, macho "real Americans," who seemed to believe Jesus would today be a chapter president of the NRA; I couldn't join ranks with Newt Gingrich's hypocritical, dim-witted "normal Americans," denying their own divorces and relatives and marching backward into the social dictatorship of the fifties. I had become such an unreal and abnormal citizen by last spring, I couldn't even include myself in Bill Clinton's compromising "moderate Americans," driving down a middle-of-the-road somewhere between Jesse Helms and Archie Bunker, becoming an ever more silent majority in the absurd administration of Don't Ask, Don't Tell.

It was hardly a surprise to feel politically abnormal, since I have a long history of life in the margins. I've never managed to prove myself an entirely normal American although, God knows, I've tried. The data governing my life are so complicated, so far outside the either/or choices offered on most surveys, I have been rejected by almost every automated system I've attempted to enter. Ten years ago, my tax return popped out of IRS computers in Connecticut because it was impossible, according to my auditor, for a single person with two dependents to live in Greenwich on my reported income. My auditor informed me I was too poor to be real. I would have been happy to pay any late taxes if he'd found a pile of money somewhere I'd forgotten to report, but his rigorous search yielded none. He couldn't believe my sons and I had existed for a year on less than Leona Helmsley, my neighbor in the back country who said "Only the little people pay taxes," had spent on one dinner party. My life didn't compute, yet there I sat, inhaling and exhaling right next to him, improbable as I was.

After I moved to New York I had to spend a day retrieving my car from the towing pound, where I learned that real

New Yorkers knew the parking regulations for every Manhattan street even if somebody had removed the signs. My postnuclear family was rejected by the computers at Princeton when the standardized financial aid forms for college loans asked either/or questions that didn't apply to me. I explained us in the margins but the forms kept getting returned—ERROR: ANSWER NOT FOUND! And whenever I called the automated customer service at my bank or credit-card company, my questions were never among the options for "press 1" or "press 2." I had to listen to the entire message and then "wait for an operator to assist you." If I were more entrepreneurial, I could probably hire myself out as a consultant: Bug Detector—If there's a kink in your system, it will find me.

Even when I was born again, I came out on the margins. A CAT scan toward the end of my coma revealed a pattern of "'irregular' brain waves," as Dr. Kalman Watsky delicately broke the news to my sister Regina. (Regina, my main companion during those nine speechless days, refused to hear the CAT scan report as bad news. "Don't worry," she assured Dr. Watsky. "'Irregular brain waves' are probably normal for my sister—she's been irregular her whole life.") After Betty Edie's memoir, *Embraced by the Light*, hit the best-seller list five years after my book, *Wake Me When It's Over*, became a near-death experience for the sales department at Random House, a friend remarked that I had "probably been ahead of the times." I doubted that. When the devoutly Christian Edie had her near-death experience, she saw God and experienced overnight, miraculous changes in her life. When I had mine, I dreamed about my ex-husband and woke up with a lot of thinking and striving to do. Whose heaven would *you* want to go to?

My sense of marginality was aggravated last spring when my applications for health insurance were rejected by three national companies, all for the same reason: I had what they called a "preexisting condition." First a condition exists and then, if you happen to get bounced from a group health plan, it starts "preexisting." This time I entered a very wide margin—along with 39 million uninsured Americans, we were practically a mainstream all by ourselves. This is a pretty big population to get "disappeared" from the press during the health care debate—especially since we were the reason it was happening at all—but this is America.

To reverse early polls showing the majority favored a single-payer plan, the national insurance lobby spent extravagant sums on a media campaign to persuade the public that uninsured citizens were too expensive to care about—a huge job, since practically everybody in the country knew somebody stuck in this unhappy category. Thirty-nine million Americans have a lot of brothers and sisters and aunts and uncles, not to mention dozens of friends and colleagues who genuinely do care about us. We obviously could not be identified.

How did the insurance lobby turn the very knowable Us into a publicly anonymous Them? Again, it was a triumph of public relations: two people who didn't exist at all—they were actors hired to play Harry and Louise, with fake histories and fictional worries—read scripts full of distortions about how much grimmer their lives would be if the dreaded Canadian Plan ever came here. Despite a surreal health care system where everybody is only one diagnosis away from preexistence, Harry and Louise convinced television viewers that my fate could never be theirs, that millions of uninsured people too stupid or lazy to take personal responsibility for themselves would be a financial burden to those who do, and that while insurance companies might be a little worried about profits disappearing with a single-payer plan, their first concern—practically their *only* concern—was for you, your favorite doctor, and certainly, your children. For an anxious middle-class, the commercial propaganda successfully replaced the facts of actual life with the virtual reality of Harry and Louise. Meanwhile, television news coverage supplied no information to contradict the distortions broadcast in the ads—when the insurance lobby is buying a lot of expensive TV time, there are plenty of other issues to fill up the news hour. Taking the gaming view of politics once more, the media covered the health care debate like a horse race—who's winning, who's losing; would Dole block Clinton, could Hillary take the Capitol; who were the brains behind the Democratic strategy; who looked good in the Republican defense; who's being embarrassed by whom. Consequently, the issues facing "we Americans" became invisible in the dominant coverage of the Beltway games.

At first, I naturally resented the label assigned to me and spent a lot of time trying to prove to the medical establishment that I was, in fact, an actual existing person: I had a birth certificate, a Social Security number, a blood type, several diplomas—I was not only here, I had two children who were also here because of me. Eventually, however, I came to embrace this label. It explained everything. Maybe the vast sense of unreality I felt was because I was not actually existing but preexisting. Maybe I'd never fully awakened from that coma. Maybe I wasn't really living yet—maybe I was in some kind of practice run at life, a training period before the real thing started.

"America, love it or leave it!" a heckler shouted to comedian Barry Crimmins in the middle of a routine mocking witless patriots.

"I would," Crimmins shouted back, "but then I'd have to live under America's *foreign* policy."

I could neither love the America I presently inhabited nor could I leave it—since our books and music and jeans and hamburgers and guns and attitudes are by now part of every civilization, there's no escape from the U.S.A. anywhere on the globe. Every time I visited my brother Paul in Ottawa, I felt the urge to apologize to his Canadian friends. American politics takes up enormous space in their country's newspapers and airtime—whether we're debating abortion, welfare, health care, gun laws, death penalties, school prayer, or family values, we're a hard country to tune out. I always imagine it must seem to our polite northern neighbors like they're living next door to the Louds. For better or worse, we are all planetary citizens now.

As the conquest mentality of U.S. soldiers, arms dealers, party politicians, and business leaders spread our native depression around the world, my border problems with the news became more and more international: wealthy investors were playing Masters of the Universe with market-driven capitalism, crushing health and welfare programs for all the "little people" paying taxes against whopping national debts—$500 billion in corporate welfare to bail out the Texas S&L speculators alone; hostile takeovers by corporate raiders were leaving millions of workers suddenly jobless, with the remaining employees too fearful to protest overtime hours and shrinking wages; and armed terrorists in every country, invoking the name of every imaginable god, were vowing death to their perceived enemies, leaving tiny, incinerated corpses in Oklahoma and unveiled girls shot down on the streets of Algeria. "The terrorist lives for terror, not the change he tells himself he wants," as novelist Louis L'Amour wrote. "He masks his desire to kill and destroy behind the curtain of a cause." All around the world, fundamentalist religious leaders and slogan-shouting patriots were marching the faithful into the ninth level of Dante's inferno.

Given the daily rap sheet on our mortal affairs, I understood why readers with malfunctioning damping apparatuses blamed the media for reporting more bad news than the human psyche is equipped to handle. But while my imperfect profession—compromised by corporate interests and passing off public relations as truth—could be fairly criticized for masking the causes of global violence and corruption, it's ultimately not all the bad news that is so disturbing. Innocent bystanders today are depressed because we have to live with too much bad behavior. We have long passed the point where not knowing about it can provide any relief. Clinging to innocence when the country's in crisis, in fact, will only prolong the suffering.

Despite the feeling of powerlessness, every citizen in the body politic has a vital function to perform. We Americans consist of approximately 250 million living cells, each occupying one of the four social roles author Cynthia Ozick defined as the perpetrators, victims, rescuers, or—the vast majority of us—the bystanders. While the power of the perpetrator, the suffering of the victim, and the heroics of the rescuer at first seem to dwarf the significance of the bystander, whose job is simply to witness, the bystanders' cultural role might be the most important of all. This is the great majority who must support, or reject, every crazy idea that comes along. Nothing becomes reality without our consent. It is the bystanders who ultimately determine what passes for "normal" in a culture.

The paradox in every society, as English philosopher David Hume observed several centuries ago, is that while populations submit to their leaders, power nevertheless always resides with the masses. "Ultimately the governors, the rulers, can only rule if they control opinion—no matter how many guns they have. This is true of the most despotic societies and the most free," MIT professor Noam Chomsky noted. "If the general population won't accept things, the rulers are finished."

When times are good—harvests plentiful and moods

generous—the bystander role is easy, even fun: we turn out for parades, take out thirty-year mortgages, eat fried chicken at church picnics. Far harder on the bystanders' psyches are the bad times, when social suffering provokes a crisis of conscience in those who must support it. During these stressful periods, it's mainly the bystanders who are vulnerable to political depressions—the others being too busy issuing orders, staying alive, or running soup kitchens. While dispirited citizens may try to protect themselves by turning the channel and tuning out bad news, this failure to witness signals a serious problem in the body politic. As the patrons in Big Dan's Bar made excruciatingly clear more than a decade ago, it's impossible to maintain innocence when a crime is in progress.

Everyone in Big Dan's had a choice to make that night: several men and women ignored the screams and conducted business as usual, mixing drinks and ordering pitchers of beer; nine men cheered the rapists on; a few disturbed patrons left the bar in revulsion; one man eventually became a witness for the prosecution. In this little microcosm of America, Hume's theory of power is provocatively obvious: without the consent of the witnesses, whether actively or passively given, the perpetrators could not proceed. Rather than being powerless, the bystanders to every social event invariably influence the outcome.

As more and more of us become numb with the bystander blues, Americans today are exhibiting the same unfocused ennui Walter Lippmann found so disturbing in his contemporaries. "The bewildered herd," as he labeled the blindly obedient citizens of the forties and fifties, didn't notice the dawning of the nuclear age. How can the silent majority raise the bar of what passes for normal today if we fail to "sustain the gaze," as author Joanna Macy described the duty of the bystander? What will it take to wake up a country in a coma, revive the deadened cells in the body politic walking like zombies through our streets?

If my personal metanoia took a nine-day coma, a six-month recovery, and another decade of continuous thinking and striving, what would produce a national metanoia, the collective will to amend all the daily habits that produce our shocking headlines? With our current politicians in a protracted state of arrested development, salvation depends on the bystanders asserting their power. Given the massive disinformation campaigns and the dizzying political spin, how can the bewildered herd become knowledgeable enough to take the lead?

"Fathers and teachers I ponder, 'What is Hell?'" Dostoevski asked, then answered: "I maintain it is the suffering of being unable to love."

While Beltway outsiders may be stunned to discover how unserious most politicians are about the beliefs they profess in the name of "we Americans," party insiders would no doubt be surprised by how passionately we believed them, how hurtful it is when patriotism is betrayed. I remember all those thousands of times I stood in my school uniform next to my desk, my hand over my heart and facing the flag, reciting the Pledge of Allegiance. I've never understood the whole contentious debate about school prayer—we had a prayer, a divinely secular plea for "liberty and justice for all," until it became meaningless.

After a girlhood full of lumps in my throat, I now get stalled every few words when I try to say the Pledge of Allegiance. All the headlines sandbagged in the backwater of my consciousness seem to seep through whenever I assume the position at stadiums or convention centers, contemplating the flag and "the republic for which it stands." The stirring image of four brave soldiers raising Old Glory on Iwo Jima isn't there anymore . . . I try not to think about the soldiers in the Okinawan courtroom today, what they stand for, what it means for us Americans. To muster any allegiance, I find it's essential to keep my mind blank through that line.

Yet invariably, my boundaries obliterated, the three marines easily advance beyond reason into my whole nervous system, fanning out grief to a twelve-year-old girl on the other side of the globe, her irrevocably altered life, her traumatized family; provoking anguish for three mothers here, who lost their boys against the terrible odds for the "conquest mentality," who will feel the ache again and again whenever they search their sons' faces for someone they loved once, desperate to find something they could love again.

I am mute by the time I reach "justice for all," stopped by the realities in the Other America, the poor nation living on the street outside my door. Since our current republic stands for profit and celebrity and only the bottom line matters, whatever the cost to the planet and its people, I lose a little more allegiance every time I read the papers. In a country where mentally ill people are homeless or jailed, where good citizens have to go blind through their cities, where the bystanders are persuaded not to care about each other . . . no, this is not "compassion fatigue." This is Dostoevski's hell.

After two months of research and field work, I had some faces, some stories, a lot of alarming facts. But I obviously didn't have the whole picture, because each shocking piece of truth I had collected still held such power to hurt. Working late one night last spring, my deadline imminent and no real intelligence to report, I was triple-reading sentences without grasping any meaning. I stopped, abruptly, suddenly overwhelmed by a tidal futility. I stared at the copious notes and highlighted clips piled high on my desk, a formidable range of paper Alps I couldn't see my way across. In two days the magazine would be "going to bed," as they say in the publishing biz, so there was no possibility of extending my deadline. My mission was looking impossible.

I tried to steady my rising anxiety by remembering the

great lesson of 1984: If nobody dies, it's not an emergency. But a people were dying, right outside my office, and if my beloved country continued its reckless habits of "unfortunate incidents" and "friendly fire" and "compassion fatigue," thousands more would die. I understood during this mind flood why therapists recommend establishing some distance from the news, why the Serenity Prayer came to be the national mantra for these trying times. But neither boundaries nor surrender can comfort the politically depressed. The only prayer for us—the Strident and Hysterical Prayer, I suppose—is to find the courage to change the small things we can, the political clout to change the big things we cannot accomplish alone, and the wisdom to know the job will never be done.

That night, reeling from all the noxious facts I'd absorbed, I knew it was time to head for Key West, as it were, or risk keeling over once more. Before I could unzombie myself and become a functioning witness again, I first had to see the big picture, find my place in the body politic. I leveled the Alps on my desk and put all my frantic notes and clips into a portable cardboard file. After adding the bulging accordion file of radioactive stories I didn't know how to dispose of—my own personal garbage barge, of sorts—I sealed the carton and labeled it the Blue Box. I then wrote a dozen personal letters to the people who immediately start worrying that I'm in another coma whenever I don't answer the phone, promising a forwarding address as soon as I had one. Before unplugging and packing my computer, I quickly finished off the questionnaire from the *Women's Review of Books* I'd stalled on that morning. ("Number 3: The funniest/best time I've had in the past six months was . . .") I then sat down with a clipboard and wrote an extravagantly long letter, by hand, to my editor, explaining why she shouldn't expect a think piece from me any time soon.

I needed some time to repair my damping apparatus, I

said—I didn't think someone who couldn't even recite the Pledge of Allegiance anymore had any business writing about American politics. I didn't know how she'd have to explain it in-house, but since I couldn't get through the newspaper without tearing up every day, it wouldn't be a lie to say I was taking a leave to go dry out somewhere. I could neither love my country nor leave it . . . what choice did I have? For anyone who takes politics as personally as I do, I had to recover my faith that "we Americans" could somehow become the country we promised to be, a republic we all could stand.

This was likely to take longer than two days. There was no chance I'd be home in time for bed, I wrote. She shouldn't wait up.

I PLEDGE ALLEGIANCE TO
THE FLAG OF THE UNITED
STATES OF AMERICA . . .

◆

PART ONE

A United State
of Denial

I

Sirens and Prayers

I SPENT MOST of my last night in New York on the phone, fielding questions from friends about the soundness of my plans—or, more accurately, my nonplans. By 2 A.M., I was wrapping up my last call to a friend in North Carolina when he suddenly asked, with audible alarm: "Good God—what was *that?!*"

"What was what?" I'd said.

"That loud noise—that blast!"

I stopped to listen and recognized the familiar wail of sirens roaring down Cathedral Parkway—maybe police cars, ambulance vans, fire trucks, rescue squads . . . who knew? His question rattled me—not because there were sirens on my street in the middle of the night but because I no longer heard them. Responding to sirens, and performing the rituals they initiated, had been a regular habit since early childhood.

My father had inducted me into siren duty some forty years ago, shortly after our family moved into a neighborhood near Resurrection Hospital in northwestern Chicago.

I remember walking home from an errand with him, still in the "Why?" stage of youth, full of questions, when the wail of an approaching ambulance interrupted our conversation. He let go of my hand briefly, made the sign of the cross, and muttered a few words to himself. My Irish Catholic family had prayers and patron saints for everything—you invoked St. Christopher before turning the ignition key to reduce risk of collisions and asked St. Blaise, before biting into a drumstick, to keep bones out of your throat. So I made the sign of the cross, too, and asked him the words to the siren prayer. Uncustomarily, he hedged. It didn't have to be a specific prayer, he said. It was fine, in emergencies, just to make one up.

"Every time you hear a siren it means somebody's in trouble—somebody's sick or had an accident," he said. "You just take a minute to think about them, ask God to send them extra strength and grace."

I naturally asked why we had to pray when the people inside the ambulance were the ones who needed help. And why didn't God, who was supposed to know everything going on everywhere in the world, just automatically send some down here? My father patiently explained that most folks struggling for oxygen were too busy to think about grace, and every siren was a reminder that, even if it wasn't coming for you this time, your number would be up sooner or later. As I understood my father's position, when trouble came, you got in it together.

He'd assured me many times that God heard every prayer we said—which I found hard to believe, since millions of Catholics in other countries were making simultaneous pleas in Chinese or Spanish, and I had trouble enough—competing with four siblings—getting my mother's attention in plain English. But that morning I got the distinct impression that these made-up prayers, offered right from the street without authorized indulgences, went straight through without delay or clerical interference.

My father had the gift of faith in abundance—a genuine, tested, beautiful certainty in the existence of God. My mother and several of my siblings have it too. I was a born doubter, and even as a child had difficulty accepting that it was St. Blaise who'd kept me alive through Thanksgiving dinner. Twelve years of parochial education did not persuade me to put the power of prayer above other possible explanations of fate: if you thought about choking to death before every meal, wouldn't that necessarily make you a more careful eater? Thinking about head-on collisions before taking the wheel could make you a more cautious driver, no? Was it St. Christopher or the fear of death that got me where I was going? Did it matter?

Being a doubter in my outsized, devoutly Catholic family was like having a bad case of vertigo and traveling with the Flying Wallendas. Although I practiced my religion for nearly two decades, sometimes rigorously, it never moved beyond practice into actual faith. Unable to contemplate the Divine—my mind invariably drew a blank there—I leaned toward expressions of faith I could see and do.

I got behind the Corporal Acts of Mercy with zeal: Feed the hungry, clothe the naked, shelter the homeless, visit the sick . . . here was a pedestrian spirituality I could grasp, a kind of candy-striper devotion mere mortals could accomplish. My father's lesson that morning fell into this category of doable faith. Ever since, the plaintive wail of a siren would make me stop for a moment, think about people in trouble, send them a wish for continued survival. As the daughter of a banker with a bleeding heart, I was probably genetically predisposed to live on the margins of "normal Americans."

The direction of civilization by 1995 had made it virtually impossible to continue this old family habit. Making up prayers would have to become a round-the-clock job. Since the sirens in New York City never stopped, I had stopped hearing them. By last spring, the electrifying shocks that usually jump-started my thinking—those "moments of being" that prompted the desire to explain, to Ask and Tell—were having exactly the opposite effect. Instead of being juiced by the news, I felt numbed by the slammer headlines contained in the Blue Box.

Reports on the O.J. verdict, the Susan Smith trial, the myriad CIA deceptions had dropped into my mind like nuclear bombs—brilliantly illuminating the insanity of our civilization for a brief seconds before the enormous clouds of disinformation rose up, the sickening fallout of excuses and lies came raining down. Despite the huge quantities of ink poured over these stories, a few months later only their shadows remained, imprinted like graffiti outside our social and political institutions while nothing much inside had changed.

With another election on the immediate horizon, another roster of "lesser evils" to consider, the prognosis for politically depressed canaries looked especially grim. It was my job to pay attention, absorb the shocks, identify their meaning—but instead of naming that tune I was tuning out completely, becoming ever more deaf and dumb. Talk about a crispy critter—I'd grown so numb to the emergencies all around me, sirens had become white noise. I no longer noticed calls for help that were audible five hundred miles away.

There were other signs, of course, that I had ceased being of much use. Steadily losing interest in the basic amenities of polite company, I had become a seating problem for friends hosting dinner parties. When conversations turned to politics—and anything from "Hello, how are you?" to "Who is your health carrier?" could get me there in a hurry—I became either strident and hysterical or mute with incredulity. Generally a solo guest, I often found myself placed at the end of the table next to the sweet, unfailingly accommodating spouse of an important person. Even with these experienced specialists in dinner-party relations, however, I could go from appetizers to dessert without finding neutral ground. The "lite" conversations we were supposed to maintain became poignant silences by coffee, interrupted periodically to exchange a sugar bowl or creamer with an excess of courtesy.

Canaries suffering the fumes of a toxic culture are not a pretty picture, and we should probably forgo dinner invitations altogether until the air clears. We become provocatively earnest, as my friend David complains, annoying the shit out of everybody. After working in the Other America for a few months, Jonathan Raban felt like he'd become "a walking mailbox for muttered stories about lost wives, lost children, lost bus fares, lost jobs, hunger and thirst." On his way to a farewell dinner before he finally got out of town, he handed a ten-dollar bill through a cab window to stop the pitch from a panhandler in a yarmulke. Ten dollars—plus cab fare to a driver who called him "a dumb motherfucker"—just so he wouldn't have to carry another impossible story through the evening. Taking a high-speed elevator up to his friends' elegant apartment, he did not feel quite grounded the rest of the night. The Air People, as he named the population living above the street people, did not get his jokes. He couldn't appreciate theirs.

Every writer obsessed with depressing realities knows we are totally draining types to have around. Most of us are rational people—we know ten dollars, or even 3,500 words, is not going to change anybody's life. But until we can supply some meaning to what we are witnessing, we are doomed to reel from the resonances. When people with bleeding hearts start throwing money out the window, it appears reckless or irrational to those who prefer to keep it in banks. Give them a terminal diagnosis, however, and most become similarly inclined to lighten their load. In the end, we all finally come to the same reality. It's too bad that it sometimes takes a brain tumor to see the big picture, especially for Air People who never touch down.

My vague agenda was to return to the Midwest to work for a while, relieve my sense of alienation by connecting with my roots. I was not so delusional as to believe going back to the heartland would cure me, or that midwesterners were inherently kinder and gentler than coastal Americans— though we do represent, in the minds of many politicians, the quintessentially innocent bystander. My urban migrations over the past two decades had relieved me of most of my innocence. By now, it was no longer a shock to discover that my city was not Oz, my neighbors were not the Waltons, my world was not without end. But I was still one of the Plains People—I periodically needed a clear horizon to regain my equilibrium.

I remember the sweltering heat last June when I pulled my ancient Volkswagen Rabbit convertible up to the curb where Estaban, the morning doorman, was waiting next to my gear. He helped me put the top down before we began loading the car with my computer and files, several duffel bags, some cherished books, and a collection of tapes. Noticing the quantity of luggage—I tend to overpack when I'm uncertain of the climate or agenda—he said it looked like he wouldn't be doing the Rabbit-watch for a while. Among his many volunteer services, Estaban kept a vigilant eye on my car and rang my bell whenever I fell behind in Alternate-Side-of-the-Street Parking. In this Manhattan game of musical chairs, apartment dwellers dart from their cubicles outfitted in slippers and sweatpants, sometimes bathrobes and shaving cream, sprint to their cars, and drive maniacally around the block, threatening and honking at other players who manage to finesse a coveted legal space.

If you sleep through this daily exercise—which I had been doing with ever greater frequency that spring—you risked a trip to the towing pound, where you encountered the most misanthropic employees in the Department of Parking Violations. For anyone who's been there, it's a bonding experience. "Ever been towed?" is a common New York inquiry that distinguishes veterans from new recruits, the same way "Ever been flooded?" is the defining question for townspeople along the banks of the Mississippi.

Outsiders who observe the frazzled drivers hurling insults at each other might find this behavior offensive, but it's probably necessary to high-strung natives. In the pressure cooker of Manhattan, most of us have either just left or are on our way to some emergency, real or imagined. I have been in this position so many times myself, late on a deadline or worried about a late kid, desperately needing someone to be mad at—why not the son of a bitch who takes the last parking space? If we didn't periodically vent our mounting tensions on this densely crowded island, I'm sure more of us would be dead.

I thanked Estaban for his vigilance that month and said he was right, I wouldn't be playing the parking games for a while.

"How long you be gone?" he asked in his heavy Dominican accent.

I wasn't sure, I told him. "A month, maybe two . . . my timetable's a little fuzzy." He tilted his head and gave me a familiar, faintly diagnostic squint.

"So where you are going this time?" he asked. "Maybe L.A.? Write about O.J.?" Under any other circumstance, I might have recognized something to be happy about: I was not on assignment to follow up on the Trial of the Century.

"I'm going to work in the Midwest, where I was born," I said. I didn't tell him I'd lost my fix on all horizons and needed the clarity of Lake Michigan. Nor did I mention the nausea that began with the newspaper, the morning sickness that could last all day. In a rare display of brevity, I summarized my destination in Estaban's language: "I'm going back to my country for a while. To see my people."

"That's good—very good," he said, nodding approval. "Everybody need that."

He gave me construction-work updates and advice about the best routes to the bridge as he loaded my computer into the backseat, then asked whether I was planning any stops on my way out of town. Just at the mailbox, I said. He raised a cautionary finger and reminded me not to park anywhere in the city with the top down, as if I didn't know that would immediately sever any attachment I had to my tape deck and computer, not to mention the Rabbit itself. Estaban often addressed me, with all due respect, as if I were slightly moronic. This was not an uncommon experience for midwesterners in New York.

That morning, however, he had every reason to question the acuity of my brain. Doormen notice everything, and the grapevine among the staff in my building has never been subdued by privacy concerns. I was sure, therefore, Estaban knew not only that he had buzzed me awake several times to save the car that week, but that Omar had smelled the muffins burning before I did, Jose found the key I'd left in my mailbox, and Rubin had retrieved the basket of laundry I'd forgotten in the dryer and placed it outside my doors, a towel draped discreetly over my folded underwear.

I lowered his finger, promising to use the mail drop on 105th Street so I wouldn't even have to get out of the car. He wasn't assured, reminding me the post office was on 104th Street.

"Estaban, don't worry—I won't even go to the bathroom till I'm out of New Jersey," I said.

"Then you better put that in the back," he said, pointing to the large thermos of coffee he'd placed next to the driver's seat. We laughed.

I put a cooler of fruit and cheese in the front while Estaban hoisted the last box from the curb. "Where does this go?" he asked, still smiling incongruously as he held the Blue Box.

I suppressed a sudden wave of panic. Where *did* it go? Even two yards away, sealed securely in sturdy cardboard, the shocks in this box had a kryptonic effect on me. All the hurts, the psychic wounds, the family secrets of the body politic kept leaking into my own life. How could I treat it, contain it, put it where it wouldn't cause further pain? "It is or will become a revelation of some order," Woolf promised, but first I had to "make it real by putting it into words . . . make it whole." In the meantime, it made me woozy with Weltschmerz.

"I don't know . . . that's the *whole problem,*" I said. "I don't know where it goes." I stood paralyzed on the curb.

Estaban wedged the box into the narrow trunk that I then locked, wondering why I was securing this grief while my music was in the open seat. Why not let a thief relieve me of the blues?

I hugged Estaban good-bye and then he stepped back, still holding my shoulders, to study my face for a moment. He frowned.

"Miss Mary Kay . . ." he said with obvious concern as a siren approached, then shouted above the roar, ". . . *YOU BE OKAY?*"

"*I'LL BE OKAY,*" I yelled back. He shouted more advice about routes, I hollered my thanks and loud affection. He opened the car door then and I got behind the wheel.

While St. Christopher is the official in charge of traffic accidents, I wasn't having apprehensions about head-on collisions that morning. My fear was of getting stalled, indefinitely, with the toxic waste in my trunk. With a thousand miles of solo driving and thinking ahead, conditions were ripe for aggravated despair. I fastened my seat belt and addressed my worries to St. Jude, the specialist in hopeless cases. How was a badly hemorrhaging canary supposed to tow a garbage barge, with or without grace?

I aimed the car south through the construction on Columbus Avenue, already missing Estaban. New Yorkers become extraordinarily attached to their doormen, whose paid employment is doing favors for people: holding doors, hailing cabs, greeting tenants, announcing visitors, receiving messengers, safeguarding children, giving directions, being useful. Doormen are the burly candy-stripers of Manhattan, performing corporal acts of mercy all day long. Routinely doing nice things has a salutary effect on the human disposition. Beloved by their tenants, doormen feature prominently in stories about what's good in New York, whenever city editors feel the need to balance bad news. Their occasional fits of self-importance are quickly forgiven because, in truth, they *are* important to a population under siege.

So what happens to the psyche of people paid to enforce "personal responsibility" all day—who have to turn off the electricity of senior citizens, evict families who fall behind on their rent, threaten custody suits to ex-wives who need child support, issue pink slips at Christmas to increase fourth-quarter dividends? People who are paid to say over and over, "Look, it's not *my* responsibility . . . I'm just following procedure"—are they the zombies walking down Broadway, detached from all feelings because it's too painful to witness the results of our daily work orders?

Kurt Vonnegut explored this question in a novel he never finished about a therapist stationed at Auschwitz. "His job was to treat the depression of those members of the staff who did not like what they were doing," he said. "My point was that workers in the field of mental health at various times in different parts of the world must find themselves asked to make healthy people happier in cultures and societies which have gone insane." He hastened to add that "the situation in our own country is nowhere near that dire. The goal here right now, it seems to me, is to train intelligent, well-educated people to speak stupidly so that they can be more popular." He gave Michael Dukakis and George Bush as examples. If he ever finishes the novel, he can add Bill Clinton and Bob Dole. Rhodes scholars and Yale graduates, learning to think like Ronald Reagan.

Many novelists have tackled this theme of communal anomie among the bystanders in berserk societies. In *One Hundred Years of Solitude*, Gabriel Garcia Marquez inflicts a whole town with a disorder that slowly causes everyone to lose their memory. They start putting labels on everything—"chair," "table," "mother"—before language goes completely and meaning is lost altogether. Unimaginable as it may seem, this science-fiction disorder is actually happening in Manhattan today. You see people wearing signs with all kinds of alarming messages, but the words aren't registering anymore. These placard holders are by now such standard fixtures on city streets, pedestrians walk by them without notice, as if they are human fire hydrants.

It's quite a stretch for fiction writers today to invent stories that would be more fantastic than our current reality. Therapists practicing in my neighborhood these days must feel like characters in a Vonnegut novel. One psychotherapist who practices here said his clients take politics very personally, "especially people with young children. One person I'm seeing now comes to mind. He's well put together, not a crazy guy, who has the feeling that the world is coming to an end. Everything he lived for in the sixties and seventies has disappeared."

After the last national election put the Contract on America in motion, the Metro section of the *Times* ran the headline "Political Depression Hits Brunch Belt." The story reported that "the Upper West Side, with its well-educated population, its bookstores and bagel shops, its older, lefty intellectuals and younger, upwardly mobile families, has long felt itself in the vanguard of social justice." Still advocating a government that takes civic responsibility, costly as it is, they are "opposed to the Zeitgeist" and have been cast as "the enemies of normal Americans" by the Gingrich regime. In dozens of interviews with this silenced majority, "the same adjectives kept surfacing: upset, distressed, disgusted, depressed, frightened, appalled."

"I'm more depressed than anyone," said Dr. Kent Sepkowitz, who spent his childhood in Oklahoma. "The only consolation I have is that I grew up during the McCarthy era, and there was life after that." Another doctor walking through Riverside Park acknowledged that while he was likely to profit financially during the Republican revolution, it didn't cheer him. "I don't mind doing better, but when I think of what's going to happen to this city, I don't have an optimistic outlook." Most of my neighbors favor a doorman culture for America, voting for candidates who promise to spread courtesies and generosity around evenly. The higher maintenance fees would be worth it here, where walking down the streets is becoming ever more precarious and depressing.

After the camp-guard faction won the election with promises to cleanse America with more prisons and death penalties, the bystander blues swept my neighborhood like the flu. This particular strain afflicted individually successful people who couldn't enjoy winning with loaded dice. I was actually heartened by news of the West Sider Depression. If more and more alienated people took the position that when trouble comes, you got into it together, maybe we actually would. I started a list of new bumper stickers— "My Country, Right and Wrong"—for West Siders headed left of the Zeitgeist, forging new frontiers, perhaps forming independent parties. There are so few political pioneers left in America, millions of voters jumped on Ross Perot's band-wagon before the Leader of the Lost Patrol ground to a halt without leaving Texas.

It takes a lot of energy to oppose the Zeitgeist, however, and energy is the first thing to go with the blues. A few years ago, my friend Barbara Neely and I were on our way home after spending a glorious month at Hedgebrook Farm, a writers' retreat on Whidbey Island in Washington. It had taken us both a few days to adjust to the quiet, contempla-tive life after arriving from Boston and New York—before we recalibrated, we were still talking at 78 rpm around a dinner table programmed for 33 rpm. Reentry was even harder, since we'd both shed any desire to fit back into civi-lization as we knew it.

The pacific beauty of the island, the company we kept, the work we did had changed us that month. These cultivated changes would suffer some erosion under the pounding forces of civilization—it would take a fierce determination and sturdy self-esteem to withstand the demands of confor-mity. On the way to the Seattle airport, I pointed to a har-bor exit marked "Marginal Way."

"That's the place for us," I said. "About as far left as you can go without being underwater." A few seconds later, we both saw another sign and started laughing: "West Mar-ginal Way."

"Left of marginal?" Barbara asked. "*That's* the place for us."

II

Psyched Out

BY THE TIME the epidemic of political depression hit the brunch belt, I had been battling with symptoms for some time. I must have been particularly vulnerable, because despite the insider information I had after covering both nominating conventions for the last presidential election, I still let some of the campaign slogans speak to me, as it were. After so many despairing months of "U.S.A. Kicks Butt," I was fairly needy for the "People First" promises of the guy from "A Place Called Hope."

For a brief time after the election, I could usually count on having a good grip on my mental health for the first hour after rising. For one thing, I had actually gotten out of bed—and since sleep is my narcotic of choice, this action alone represented a triumph of will. Though most of my brain cells were still in a slow stretch to consciousness in that dreamy first hour, my family knew this was the time to ask for the car, for advances on allowances, for apologies or for-giveness over unsettled scores. The quality of my mercy was not yet strained. I was generally able to convince myself, especially if I began preparing a breakfast of fiber and bananas, that I would live up to all the expectations a sane and responsible person faces in a normal day. I was even able to believe in the concept of "normal." Then, inevitably, it was time to go to work. I opened the newspaper.

I would begin my job of reading and thinking about civilization, shepherding wild facts from all directions and taming them into some kind of domestic order for people busy doing other jobs in banks and schools and zoos. By the time I had ingested the whole of the *New York Times*—which pledges itself to report "All the News That's Fit to Print"— my hope that simply electing a new administration could relieve us of further traumatic headlines was seriously frayed. I remember the morning the tether line broke, and I started the free fall into the crease between the photographs on page one.

At the top, an exuberant First Lady was inspecting a splendid table set with silver, crystal stemware, and fine china for the governors' dinner at the White House that evening. A five-column story described a deliberately all-American menu: "Smoked marinated shrimp with mango horseradish chutney, roast tenderloin of beef, baby vegetables in a zucchini basket and Yukon Gold potatoes" followed by "goat cheese from Massachusetts" as well as "an apple sherbet tureen with Applejack mousse and hot cider sauce" along with vintage wines "from Virginia, California and Oregon."

The bottom photo, situated a mere five inches below the hem of the First Lady's evening gown, bore the caption: "A Brutal Day to Live Outdoors." It provided a long-distance silhouette of two homeless men huddled before a trash-can fire under the Henry Hudson Bridge. I wondered if one might be Eddie the Loop, a panhandler who worked the Fifty-seventh Street exit ramp on the West Side Highway. Whenever I drove home by that route, I paid a $1.50

toll at the bridge and then either paid another buck to Eddie—one of the self-employed windshield washers servicing unlucky motorists caught by the red light—or suffered the emotional abuse of refusing. But the two-sentence story offered no names. The homeless are the camp inmates of our cities—we know them only by their numbers. The caption mentioned freezing temperatures, with no relief in sight, but no information about the dinner menu under the bridge that night. Apparently, not fit to print.

The habit of triple-reading sentences began that year: can't be true, read it again, how can this be? Like a nervous tic that erupted under dire stress, these knocking questions would not settle down. Since my job obliged me to read enormous amounts to keep up in this rattling age of information, I couldn't afford such lengthy ruminations over each story. I started a new file, Truths with Consequences, where I stashed all the bizarre facts of the week. Unaware of the monster headache it would become, I planned to deal with it later when I had the knocking under control.

Without an organizing principle, I loosely clipped the Facts of the Week together every Friday and attached a summary page of the highlights. After two frantic paragraphs about the marinated shrimp in Washington and the trash-can dinner under the bridge, I sat on my prose and briefly reported on the first log in 1993:

> The Serbian Army has officially established the penis as a weapon by ordering its soldiers to rape the enemy, and is so far credited with 60,000 assaults on Muslim women; The U.N. investigation of Iraq's nuclear weapons is leading to speculation about how many other "developing nations" are playing with plutonium; A mentally retarded young woman in Glen Ridge, New Jersey, testifies that she was gang raped with two baseball bats and a broom

in the basement of a neighbor's house by four boys who swore "she wanted it;" A newborn infant was found in a gym bag outside a Long Island high school and was miraculously revived by nurses at Winthrop-University Hospital, who first named him "Jim" to honor his birthplace but later renamed him Christopher; The United States has a greater percentage of citizens in jail than any other developed country; To save money while awaiting trial for the Rodney King beating, Officer Laurence Powell "moved into his parents' home, where his legal papers are stacked in cardboard boxes beside his mother's collection of dolls"; The American Academy of Pediatrics reported the average American child views 18,000 televised murders before graduating from high school; According to FBI statistics, a woman is beaten every 15 to 18 seconds during a normal day in America; According to *Nation* columnist Alexander Cockburn, "on Super Bowl Sunday, a greater than normal number of women lie bleeding amid the Budweiser cans."

When my damping apparatus began malfunctioning that year, I started cheating on my job: I would skim the news about the national deficit, the Joint Chiefs' arguments against homosexuals, the Hindu "cleansing" of Muslim neighborhoods in Bombay, the tons of toxic waste the Superpowers have been dumping near the North Pole. I'd think about my immediate responsibilities to the teachers and zookeepers, of course, who might be depending on some kind of explanation. I was sure they'd heard about the Rodney King beating or the Glen Ridge trial—they might even know about the doll collection, and the baseball bats. I would imagine their hearts breaking. An explanation would be useful. I'd calculate the odds of my coming up with one by the end of the day. I would look up my horoscope. Where were the comics?

The trouble with having the bystander blues is that there's no immediate psychological treatment or cure. Since West Sider Depression is not yet recognized in the American Psychological Association's diagnostic manual, going into therapy can even be detrimental. For those of us who feel traumatized by our culture, traumatized by *news*, recovery is impossible if we start believing the trouble is all in our heads. Conventionally trained therapists might easily interpret our symptoms as a failure to separate ourselves from others; we would be encouraged to develop coping techniques to maintain more distance. In truth, our problem is we feel too separated, profoundly alienated, grieved by the denial that one life indeed affects another's. We need a therapy that will link us back up with the human family—one that goes beyond self-help and recognizes that our personal problems have deep political roots.

The truth that cultural and social realities have an indelible effect on personal mental health is the very same truth that launched Freud's brilliant career five decades ago. Professor Judith Herman, a clinical psychiatrist on the faculty of Harvard Medical School, recounts in *Trauma and Recovery* the famous story of "Anna O.," a bright but severely disturbed young woman who found such relief in telling her childhood secrets to an attentive doctor, she gave psychoanalysis the generic name we use today: "the talking cure." After documenting her story and seventeen others, Freud concluded that "hysterics suffer mainly from reminiscences." The proximate source of their painful memories were "one or more occurrences of premature sexual experience"—in some cases, with their fathers. This unanticipated discovery of childhood incest and rape was deeply troubling to Freud—for personal as well as political reasons.

Hysteria was so common in Europe in the late nine-teenth century—not only among the working classes of Paris but also among the bourgeois elite in Vienna—"that if his patients' stories were true, and if his theory were correct, he would be forced to conclude that 'perverted acts against children' were endemic," Professor Herman reported. Despite this depressing finding, Freud published "The Aetiology of Hysteria," alerting his colleagues and an unaware public to a serious social problem.

Instead of sharing his alarm that sexual crimes against children were causing a widespread, debilitating pathology, both the psychiatric community and the public condemned the bearer of bad news and accused Freud of being hysteri-cal. He quickly discovered that "no matter how cogent his arguments or how valid his observations," Herman wrote, his truth could not survive in a culture unwilling to recog-nize and act on it. Depressed and ostracized, Freud faced a terrible decision: He could stick with his truths and watch his career sink into oblivion—where his French colleague in hysteria, Pierre Janet, was currently headed—or he could reexamine his data for a more socially acceptable theory and become the Father of Psychology. He deserted Anna O. and took his place in history.

In subsequent publications Freud decided that "these scenes of seduction had never taken place . . . they were only fantasies which my patients had made up." This theory—that hysterical women should be treated as prevaricators—was greeted with such enthusiasm by the psychiatric community, Freud went on to develop even more fantastic ones. Since so many female patients entertained provoca-tive "rape fantasies," it seemed reasonable to assume all women "wanted it," however unconsciously. Penis envy did not seem at all ridiculous in these hysterical times. Once Freud had the rhythm of the social order, he was no slouch. In the legacy of Freudian psychology today, "the inferiority and mendacity of women are fundamental points of doctrine," Herman concludes. Had anyone still been listing to Anna O. by then, she might have given us another term for the evolution of psychoanalysis: the gaslight treatment.

Nearly half a century passed before a social movement strong enough to resuscitate the truth finally emerged. In 1975, *Against Our Will* shocked the world with proof of endemic rape. Susan Brownmiller was called "a militant man-hater," but wouldn't take anything back. Louise Armstrong's *Kiss Daddy Goodnight* dropped a grenade into public ignorance about incest in 1978—she was called "strident and hysterical," but she wouldn't take anything back either. And in 1980, sociologist Diana Russell published an in-depth study of more than nine hundred women, selected by scientific random sample, which asserted these stunning facts about America: one out of four women had been raped; one out of three had been sexually abused or harassed as children. By the early eighties, crisis hot lines were buzzing and shelters for battered women and children were overflowing. The "fantasy" of sexual trauma could no longer be denied as a daily reality.

In those interim five decades, of course, there were plenty of signs that the sickness and pathology of our societies were having a depressing effect on the mental health of millions of men and women. The newspapers after World War II must have been fatal for anyone whose damping apparatus was malfunctioning: 6 million Jews were tortured and murdered in concentration camps, and many "survivors" had suicidal depressions; 100,000 Japanese civilians in Hiroshima and Nagasaki were killed, with millions more irradiated by hydrogen bombs; worldwide, 24 million soldiers were dead, 12 million wounded, and uncounted millions of veterans emerged from the war with a new mental illness called "combat fatigue."

Strikingly similar to the "barbed-wire syndrome" and "shell shock" of World War I, veterans suffering combat fatigue filled up the back wards of veteran hospitals all over the world. Two American psychiatrists, J. W. Appel and G. W. Beebe, concluded in a 1946 study that 200 to 240 days in combat would produce symptoms in even the strongest soldiers—shaking hands, impaired nervous systems, numb limbs, severe depression, overwhelming guilt, and suicidal impulses. "There is no such thing as 'getting used to combat,'" Appel and Beebe concluded. "Psychiatric casualties are as inevitable as gunshot and shrapnel wounds in warfare."

That same year in Vienna, the mental-health capital of the world, the distinguished humanitarian Viktor Frankl urged his psychiatric colleagues to spend more time thinking about the human political self: How did social systems create an altered state in which decent citizens could agree to the cruel torture and murder of 6 million others? Frankl, an Auschwitz survivor, believed psychoanalysis had focused too narrowly on the private self, and argued that strictly inward-directed therapy was not much help to people traumatized by social and political institutions. Rather than stressing the pleasure principle, which Freudian theory had identified as the strongest human motivator, Frankl believed there was an even stronger one: the human will to meaning.

Through logotherapy, "the search for meaning," Frankl taught depressed clients to view their future with "tragic optimism." Tragic, because human existence will never be without the "triad of pain, guilt and death"; optimism, because by engaging the will, pain can become a means to greater compassion; guilt can become an indication of what needs to be changed; and recognition of death can become "an incentive to take responsible action." He encouraged depressed patients not to seek happiness—except for other people. "Happiness cannot be pursued; it must ensue, and only as the unintended side-effect of one's dedication to a cause greater than oneself or as the by-product of one's surrender to a person other than oneself." Logotherapy, eventually recognized as the Third School of Viennese Psychotherapy, suggested that we could never be happy as individuals until we took care of the chronic unhappiness of the body politic.

Perhaps because there were so many private cases of shell shock, hysteria, and neuroses to treat in the postwar years, Frankl's theory of "responsible action" was largely ignored as psychoanalysts delved deeper into our sexual frustrations. The civilization job was simply too big. That, at least, was my understanding some fifteen years ago, when an editor at a national women's magazine assigned me to investigate an outbreak of agoraphobia after the Three Mile Island accident.

Agoraphobia, loosely translated to mean "the fear of open spaces," is often called "the Housewives Disease" among therapists, because 95 percent of the afflicted are women. The indications are disabling panic attacks, short-ness of breath, accelerated heartbeats, and "irrational fears of imminent danger." Symptoms frequently occur after a traumatic clash with the outside world—a mugging, a rape, a nuclear meltdown. The cases at Three Mile Island were identified in the months after government vans with loud-speakers on the roofs had driven through neighborhood streets, warning the residents: "Close all windows and doors . . . Mothers, don't breast-feed your babies . . ."

My research suggested that agoraphobics were notori-ously resistant to treatment. Psychologists found them unusually imaginative, creative, and intelligent, but extremely uncooperative when it was time to "come back to reality." There just wasn't enough in it for them anymore—they were depressed, and their breasts hurt. After spending time with these highly articulate, self-imprisoned women, I found that their responses seemed perfectly rational to me. Occasionally strident and hysterical, they were taking the nuclear age exceptionally personally, the way all of us would after Energy Secretary Hazel O'Leary started opening files about what our military knew, when they knew it, how they kept exposing people to plutonium anyway. Including us Americans. But I was also aware that women's magazines are disinclined to publish bad news without offering a few upbeat suggestions.

Finally, I found one group of determined agoraphobics who were making slow but steady progress. After trying various "talking cures" which produced only temporary relief, they joined a local environmental organization and became community activists. Getting out of the house for meetings remained a challenge—any group of Agoraphobics Anonymous would necessarily have a high absenteeism rate—but rage and anger proved sturdy motivators. By connecting with others who shared their "irrational fears," they eventually shed their feelings of helplessness and regained sanity. Their experiences strongly suggested, as did the assignment I turned in, that lasting relief for agoraphobia did not occur by changing the perceptions of the women, but by changing the pathology "out there."

My editor was furious. "This solution is far too complicated for our readers," she said. "This is a *service* magazine for women. We don't do politics." Rather than providing a few quick tips that could be tried by next Tuesday—let alone by next month, when readers would be busy pursuing happiness with twelve steps to younger-looking skin—I had confounded the mental-health thing with the political thing. The information I had gathered was "far too depressing," she said. "We want readers to feel *happy* when they finish our magazine." It was my first lesson in the Valium Theory of journalism—prose should numb the blues without trying to name the problem.

* * *

Unable to follow the rewrite specifications, I let the story be "killed," as we say. I still depended on "the writing cure" that Woolf prescribed, but when conditions worsen I knew even that didn't work. Woolf, too, had periodic difficulty with her damping apparatus. When Freud's work was published by the Hogarth Press—founded by Virginia and her husband, Leonard Woolf—I wondered what she, herself a silent victim of incest, thought of his hysterical theory about her experiences. Did she feel gaslit? We know she wrestled with severe bouts of madness all her life, which accelerated as Nazi troops invaded Europe. Was her last, most devastating depression influenced by political grief? Fact-shocked and truth-fatigued, assaulted with criticism for being an "anti-patriotic" man-hater after publishing *Three Guineas* in 1938, her brilliant and impassioned argument against war, she lost her way in the search for meaning. In 1941, she filled her pockets with rocks and walked into the River Ouse.

Three decades later writer Hunter Thompson, tracking fear and loathing in American politics for *Rolling Stone* magazine, filled the trunk of his Chevrolet with "two bags of grass, seventy-five pellets of mescaline, five sheets of high-powered blotter acid, a salt shaker half full of cocaine, and a whole galaxy of multi-colored uppers, downers, screamers and laughers" and drove to Las Vegas. Kurt Vonnegut chain-smoked Pall Malls. I went to sleep in 1984 and didn't wake up for nine days. What scared the bejesus out of me: There was still no treatment for our political disease, and every thinking person I knew was having grave difficulty with their damping apparatus.

"Believe me," I told my editor when she warned me against depressing readers with the truth, "your readers *are* depressed. They'd be relieved to know they're not alone." God knows, we'd tried every other imaginable cure in the last ten years. We'd joined Alcoholics/Gamblers/Overeaters Anonymous, become Adult Children, chastised Toxic Parents. The *New York Times* reported that by the mid 1990s, Americans were participating in an estimated 100 million therapy sessions with licensed practitioners and paying approximately $8.2 billion annually, not counting prescription drugs, to relieve this national despair.

These figures didn't include all the people who were trying to feel better by holding hands and humming from the top of Machu Picchu, or jumping off bridges on bungee cords—let alone all the nameless people living under them. Nor did they include all the lonely readers who, in the privacy of their own homes, pored over books on codependence/women-who-love-too-much/men-who-hate-them, while quietly sipping or smoking themselves into oblivion. And what was the drug culture but a measure of our unremitting depression and distress? The War on Drugs had filled our prisons with poor people caught trafficking or consuming illegal self-medications on the streets, while an insomniac president was swallowing Halcion prescribed by the White House doctor to help him sleep. Valium, Prozac, Xanex, and Elavil were keeping decision makers on Capitol Hill and in corporate America calm while they drafted laws and implemented programs that made the rest of us nuts.

We'd tried to cheer ourselves up with Yukon Gold potatoes and goat cheese from Massachusetts, but there simply wasn't enough wine from Virginia, California, and Oregon to blot out the vastness of our blues. It seemed to me we had exhausted the options: Our survival—mental *and* physical—now depended on tackling the big job "out there."

... AND TO THE REPUBLIC
FOR WHICH IT STANDS ...

◆

PART TWO

A Politics Bordering on MAD

III

The Shocks in the Box

LESS THAN A year after the guy from Hope took office, I was already having difficulty holding up my end of the small talk at dinner parties. Nevertheless, I agreed to deliver a keynote lecture for a conference of female business executives in Spokane, Washington. I was one of three experts invited to address the issue of "stress"—a psychotherapist, a management consultant, and me, whose main expertise with stress was as a patient once felled by it. "If you can't be a good example," the writer Catherine Aird advised, "at least you can be a provocative warning."

Stress was so commonplace by 1993, any adult who claimed not to be experiencing large quantities of the stuff could be considered un-American. The conference brochure promised we would offer tips on managing it more efficiently, a promise that made me uneasy because I was increasingly convinced nobody should be helping people adapt to the craziness of modern life. To address the craziness itself, however, meant raising threatening questions about our families, jobs, relationships, our whole society.

Easier by far, if only temporarily, was to learn a few deep-breathing exercises.

The therapist who delivered the luncheon address described her philosophy as "eclectic—a little Freud, a little Esalen, a little New Age." She opened her remarks with the story of a depressed client who showed a lackluster effort in improving herself. "This woman was a mess," she said. "She had a negative attitude, didn't exercise regularly, and was wearing all the wrong colors." The audience, an assemblage of well-educated, mostly middle-aged executives, chuckled. They thought she was kidding about the colors.

"No, really—she was an April, and she was wearing *red*," said the therapist. "She needed to have her colors done." Starting your day in the right hue could make all the difference, she insisted, and described how her own life began soaring when she got into gold. Wearing a positive attitude and lots of gold she did, indeed, appear to be a lot happier than the rest of us. The initial incredulity gave way as the advice-hungry audience, with the exception of a few skeptical holdouts, dutifully applied pens to their conference notebooks. I hoped they were writing, "Luncheon therapist—too eclectic for me." But I suspect many entries said: "Make appointment on Monday—have colors done."

This notion that a thinking woman could relieve her depression by changing her wardrobe was a popular theme in national women's magazines, which reach more than 60 million readers a month. If new clothes didn't work, you probably needed to go on a diet or try a new haircut. As I listened to the luncheon expert and observed the response, I knew the dinner keynote I had prepared would go down like castor oil.

My talk addressed social stress, which couldn't be relieved with self-help solutions. I suggested that when reality doesn't fit, we shouldn't wear it, and spoke admiringly of the agoraphobic housewives who became community activists. They had inspired me to think about political depression as a powerful force, not something to be cured of but to be transformed into energy and used. I hoped, in fact, that more and more of us would become seriously distressed, since changing the world was going to take a lot of people and we had no time to waste. The first step in a national metanoia was to acknowledge reality, of course, which was never easy. The bulk of my time at the podium was spent alarming the audience with my facts. I concluded by quoting the poster on my office wall: "The truth will make you free, but first it will make you miserable."

Applause was modest. And, I suspect, came mainly from gratitude that I had stopped talking. I wasn't thinking, when I wrote it, that everyone would have just eaten dessert.

Early the next morning, I began a six-hour drive from Spokane to Whitefish, Montana, to catch up with the annual meeting of Journalists and Women Symposium (JAWS). Interstate 90 was a straight river of asphalt for as far as I could see, which was indeed forever in Big Sky country, and the blue/gold horizon was a 180-degree Imax Technicolor screen. Sipping coffee and coasting on cruise control, I felt the cognitive hangover I woke up with that morning finally start to lift. Aware that something had gone very wrong the night before, I paid a little hospital call on myself to diagnose exactly what it was.

I wasn't upset because my talk had offended some members of the audience—that was within the realm of normal, since it's been my job for the last two decades to provoke as many people as possible in 3,500 words or less. I was upset because I forgot that it would, forgot that when you torpedoed the traditions and institutions people are living in, you needed to fling them a lifeboat for the open seas. Whether my aim had been accurate or not, I obviously hadn't finished the job.

I didn't feel obligated to supply a happy ending—that,

ultimately, was the bystanders' duty. But as a messenger of bad news, I had an obligation to supply some meaning. I had done exactly what so infuriated me about my own profession: I had pummeled the crowd with my facts, but they were facts without context. Unanchored from their own reality, bystanders cannot become engaged, cannot feel enraged—cannot, therefore, embark upon Frankl's path of "responsible action." I had left my audience rudderless . . . because I myself didn't know what direction these facts required us to take.

In the national metanoia I kept imagining, the whole body politic would come into therapy, sit down on the couch, and face the facts in our newspapers. It would soon be apparent we Americans suffered from being fragmented, megalomaniacal, delusional, and immersed in denial. We are one nation of split realities. One fact in the newspaper—the 18,000 episodes of televised murder, let's say—has one meaning for Arnold Schwarzenegger, an actor with made-up wounds in fake wars who supports real military aggression; another for Eddie the Loop, the dismembered veteran from a real war who leads an unimaginable life under the Henry Hudson Bridge; yet another for Laurence Powell, the police officer whose boxes of legal papers were blocking his mother's view of her doll collection. Whose reality is the authentic one? Either some of us are crazy, or there is no such thing as "the real world." Or there is, but as the late physicist Frank Oppenheimer once said, "We don't live in the real world. We live in a world we made up."

Computer science calls these made-up systems—our economy, two-party politics, the military, sexual identities, race relations, religious practices—"virtual realities," because they represent what is "true" for the people inside them. The term was first coined to describe the dazzling technology used to train pilots and brain surgeons and other high-risk professionals, without having to involve actual passengers or patients. By donning specially equipped helmets and gloves that produced the sights, sounds, feel, and touch of another reality, a trainee safely seated in a classroom could be lifted twenty-five thousand feet above sea level, exposed to high winds, mountain ranges, thunderstorms, and lightning, maybe even taken through a crash landing. Game over, the pilot-to-be emerged with a lot of knowledge about what not to do next time, but without a scratch. Nobody dies.

A frequent complaint about our former president was that he was "out of touch with reality." But in fact, George Bush was deeply immersed in his own virtual reality, based on this guiding principle: "Do whatever it takes to get reelected." Because of his vision trouble, he relied on image consultants, spin doctors, focus groups, and pollsters to give him a touch and feel for "the American people." To launch him in the direction of the most votes, Republican strategists constructed a Big Tent on a narrow platform and led him through some tricky maneuvers around the truth—but lies are only a problem in political reality if they register "a bounce in the polls." That is, cause voters to think twice and change their minds.

Sometimes the lies were harmless, even amusing. When the *Wall Street Journal* asked Bush what he had been thinking about when his plane was shot down in World War II, he said: "Well, you go back to your fundamental values. I thought about Mother and Dad and the strength I got from them. And God and faith. And the separation of church and state." Was anyone else "so churlish to doubt that our man Bush was contemplating the separation of church and state as his plane hurtled toward the sea?" columnist Molly Ivins wondered. Worse still, what if he *were*?

The body politic understood that Bushspeak was the language of public relations, not truth—a luxury we'd learned by then to live without. We could almost hear his internal polling mechanism trip in that sentence: "Oops! I just mentioned God—better throw in something for the secularists." We didn't think twice. In fact, bounces were so rare in the polls, the body politic clearly wasn't mulling over every lie from Washington. Who had the time? Instead, we constructed a public reality into which noises from the Beltway insiders could be absorbed.

When pollsters called during the televised violence in Baghdad, for example, we'd been listening to the president's sound track for weeks, repeating over and over that the Gulf War was "not about the price of oil—it's about democracy and freedom." Asked if we were alarmed by this obvious lie from our president, we said no, we were quite familiar with the democracy-and-freedom thing, especially during historic moments like these. Mesmerized by the stunning weaponry shown on television, saturated with enthusiastic media reports "approved by military censors," walking through neighborhoods festooned with yellow ribbons, most of us agreed to have "confidence in the president." We even agreed to think of Kuwait as a democracy for a while.

When two or more people agree that selected absurdities are real, therapists call what we have achieved a "consentual reality." Christmas, for example: we agree that because a Virgin Mother gave birth in Bethlehem almost two thousand years ago, we should all go to the mall and buy jewelry and watches and stereo equipment. If the verbal artillery in a consentual reality is heavy enough, even the strongest independent thinkers will eventually break down—psychiatrists Appel and Beebe, as noted, estimated that for soldiers under gunfire, the breakdown occurred somewhere between 200 to 240 days.

The body politic has by now been exposed to so many years of Bushspeak and Billbabble ("I smoked marijuana once but I didn't inhale") it is possible that our hearing is now deeply impaired. My autistic friend Donna Williams, the author of *Nobody Nowhere*, once told me that a symptom of autism is that "the meaning drops out of spoken words, and I hear only 'Blah, blah, blah.'" So maybe the body politic should be tested for autism: Whenever our politicians today open their mouths, what do *you* hear?

This cognitive dissonance could explain why we didn't connect any personal meaning to political noises from Washington for the last dozen years. We knew, for example, that before becoming Reagan's running mate Bush supported abortion rights; then, nearly overnight, he became ardently antiabortion. Though he made impassioned speeches and gestures, few people accepted this spectacular moral reversal as just happening to coincide—and not being propelled by—a splendid political opportunity. We know where the horses and carts go. But we did accept this whopping lie as being within the realm of "whatever it takes." Wary of his vision thing, we nevertheless put on the helmets and gloves of the Kinder, Gentler Nation and went for a ride.

Had we known then what a gigantic cognitive hangover we'd be suffering by the end, we might have declined the ticket. But we didn't know—the consentual reality of the KGN was a monumental structure of denial. Guided by pollsters and media handlers, we numbly watched Bush ban abortions at military hospitals and clinics; pack the Supreme Court; institute gag-rules at teen counseling centers; and restrict Medicaid coverage, which in effect canceled poor women's right to abortion. When the political game crash-landed in November of 1992 and Bush stepped out of the driver's seat, nobody was supposed to be hurt.

Instead, the virtual reality that was all in our heads, meant only to advance one man's political career, had infiltrated actual lives: my sons and their friends will live the rest of their reproductive years under a Supreme Court hostile to their rights. Some will die, like seventeen-year-old Rebecca Bell, sacrificed on the political altar of parental consent laws. And some—perhaps the shivering teenager observed hiding in the bushes near the Long Island high school where baby Christopher was abandoned in a gym bag—will live with unspeakable memories from now on, maybe go to jail, because the truth about sex and choice and responsibility was gagged when our children were most desperate for it.

These disenfranchised members of the body politic— baby Christopher, his young mother, Rebecca Bell, our own sons and daughters—simply didn't show up on the polling lists: they didn't vote, didn't have phones, couldn't bounce in the polls, so they didn't exist. Our heads aching with throbbing recognition, it was tempting to fall back on the quick fix—elect a new president who promised change, hope for recovery in the next hundred days. Indeed, with a stroke of his pen on day one, President Clinton removed all the harmful gags and abortion restrictions he could. Then, preparing to lift another ban on the body politics' sexuality, he suddenly faced an angry coalition of the Joint Chiefs of Staff, medals flashing and muscles flexing, furious with him for messing up "military morale."

"The Newspaper of Record" does not like to dwell on the sensational or gritty details of sexual problems in America. In a story about a homosexual sailor on the crew of the *Belleau Wood*, beaten so viciously by two shipmates that his mother could identify her dead son only by the tattoos on his arms, the *New York Times* allowed this statement, three paragraphs down from the lead: "The Navy said that his skull was battered, that most of his ribs were broken and that his penis was cut." And that . . . *what?* The story moved brusquely on to detail ensuing legal battles, whether the case could classify as "a hate crime," whether public feelings about the military would bounce, and so on. It concluded by quoting a Navy official who was speaking for the Joint Chiefs' Chairman Colin Powell who was speaking for the Joint Chiefs who were speaking for the military brass, who all wanted the American people to know they were "closely monitoring the case." Albeit, from a distance.

When the Joint Chiefs declare a sexual-identity crisis in public, even the *Times* is motto-bound to provide some picture of it. A remarkable five-column photo, credited to "Department of Defense," pictured the six generals in full uniform seated at a conference table, their hands folded identically, right over left. Some faces were lined with wrinkles that suggested they have laughed—but here, for the public, their lips were thinned, serious, as if the Chiefs wanted to be thought of as dangerous. The wall behind them contained two framed portraits—an airborne fighter plane and some kind of field weaponry—between three magnificently draped windows, the panes concealed behind fine wood paneling.

Not a single to-do list, newspaper, coffee cup, or personal item marred the cleansed surface of the mahogany table—polished so brightly it reflected the upside-down images of the generals, their neatly aligned fingers, their stripes, medals, ties, even the Adam's apples under their chins. In this portrait of military reality, nothing candid, messy, confused, or emotional distracted from the image of united power the Chiefs meant to convey. Their pose brought to mind the words cited so often in the *Times*: "Top security . . . Military secrets . . . Army discipline . . . Navy spokesmen." I asked my sister Regina, reading over my shoulder at the kitchen table, what the photo brought to her mind. She hesitated a moment, then paraphrased a line from *Leaving Normal*, a movie we'd seen the night before: "'Please God, don't let anyone think I'm a homosexual.'"

The Chiefs had assembled in this manner to explain why they felt allowing "avowed" homosexuals into their armies would ruin military morale. That this guy Clinton "never even served in Vietnam" seemed particularly to incense them, as if serving in that war would have made him a more agreeable man. I looked again at the humorless faces of the generals. They seemed not to be making a great cosmic joke by asking us to admire and respect "military morale." Do they think we don't know?

Nowhere is the difference in our perceptions of reality more disturbing than between the Americans who plan wars and the Other Americans who serve in them. When former Defense Secretary Robert McNamara expressed regrets in his recent memoir about his role in the Vietnam War, *Harper's* editor Lewis Lapham remembered how, years ago, "McNamara explicitly defined the bombing raids that eventually murdered upwards of two million people north of Saigon as a means of communication." Entrenched in the Zeitgeist of the sixties, "he was caught up in a dream of power that substituted the databases of a preferred fiction for the texts of common fact. What was real was the image of war that appeared on the flow charts and computer screens. What was not real was the presence of pain, suffering, mutilation and death," Lapham wrote. "What do we mean by democracy if we must communicate with one another by bomb-o-gram?"

An old man now, the retired McNamara regretted his generation's arrogant power dream, which became a fatal reality for the fifty-eight thousand names inscribed on the Vietnam Memorial—half belonging to soldiers who were seventeen or eighteen years old when they died—and doomed another million and a half who survived to a haunted existence. The former Secretary described the nightmares he's had since coming to, reviewing data and decisions that turned out to be wrong, and I'm sure they are traumatic. But his postwar distress is not the same as that of the veterans who served under him. For one thing, he is still standing. For another, unlike former army nurse Diane Evans, he can safely approach a juicy beef tenderloin at a banquet table without being assaulted by sudden flashbacks of bloody human limbs. The perpetrators bear social responsibility for war, but rescuers and victims carry the weight of personal experience for the rest of their lives.

It's unlikely the bystanders who consented to the sanitized, aerial view of "the Vietnam era" would have agreed had they known what was passing for "normal" on the ground. The press didn't circulate most of the shocks in the box until twenty years later, being busily preoccupied at the time with the usual questions of who's winning, who's losing, who's embarrassing whom. Few voices at press conferences back then were asking Lapham's question: But what do these bomb-o-grams *mean?* Whenever they did, politicians and military spokesmen provided the standard reply: "Blah, blah, national security, blah, blah, democracy and freedom, blah, blah."

In October 1969, while crisply uninformed middle-aged men were holding media briefings and aiming pointers at flip charts in Washington, twenty-three-year-old Joan Furey was working twelve-hour shifts, seven days a week, at the Seventy-first Evacuation Hospital at Pleiku, South Vietnam. Like the thousands of soldiers she eventually mended or mourned, she had volunteered for duty because she believed in her country. Almost immediately, however, her patriotism was tested by the reality of her M.A.S.H. unit. Furey had served only nine months of her tour when she stopped next to the gurney of an "expectant," a badly wounded young soldier who had flunked triage that day and was expected to die soon. She was by then "sick of death," as Laura Palmer recounted in "How to Bandage a War," a memorable account of the rescuers' reality in the power dream that gripped McNamara's generation.

A mere integer in the flow charts, Furey clung desperately to the Washington conviction that America was facing a spectacular threat, even if it was impossible to discern from Pleiku. The fathers of our country would never recklessly sacrifice so many of their young—the incomprehensible danger to Cincinnati and Wichita *had* to be imminent and grave. War, of all things, could never be "just politics." But she lost her faith next to the gurney that day.

"*This* soldier is going to live," Furey decided. Ignoring the fifteen triage survivors she was responsible for keeping alive, she set up an IV and started dripping quarts of blood into the shattered remains of a boy whose preexisting condition hovered on non-:

"As she begins to unwind the field dressing, all the blood she has been pumping into the soldier suddenly pours out over her. Blood and brains, the whole back of his head, are lying in her hands. Calmly, she puts his head together and secures it neatly with a clean dressing. She's in a fugue state. Someone comes and gets her, takes her out for a cigarette," Palmer recounted. "After a couple of Parliaments, she goes back to work. The other nurses and medics don't talk about what has just taken place. Too risky."

"If you talked about it, you would feel it," Furey reflected two decades later. "And if you allowed yourself to feel, you could not have continued to do your job." After returning to civilization "she would wake up at night, desperately feeling the need to wash her hands," Palmer reported. "I felt like Lady Macbeth," Furey told her. "I couldn't get the blood of Vietnam off my hands."

During the promotional campaign for McNamara's memoir, the *Times* ran a photograph of him in Hanoi shaking the hand of another smiling old man, General Vo Nguyen Giap. Although the caption gave only the names, the dates, and the place of their conciliation meeting, their expressions seemed to say: "No hard feelings, old chap. I didn't mean those bomb-o-grams personally."

In truth, war is rarely personal for the generals and presidents who give the orders. If they exhibit symptoms of post-traumatic stress disorder at all, they might have some night sweats over miscalculations on line graphs and under-reported casualty lists. World War II veteran Bush, unless he was just kidding again, faced conundrums about the separation of church and state. But these abstract nightmares are not likely to make the dreamers sit bolt upright like seaman Joseph Gracy, his bed covers flung clear across the room, sweating profusely after washing body parts off the deck of his ship, over and over for forty years. Only nineteen when he was rescued from shark-infested waters after a kamikaze attack in World War II, he was the only survivor. "I knew these people," he said. He spent most of the subsequent decades in an alcoholic haze, wishing he hadn't.

War is never over for the veterans who come home. Symptoms of post-traumatic stress disorder—the newest label in our long history of shell shock, barbed-wire syndrome, battle fatigue, all the politically induced disorders we keep rediscovering in the aftermath of power dreams— are rarely relieved by time. Harvard Medical School psychiatrist Roger Pitman, studying data on some of the 210,000 World War II survivors who continue to suffer full-blown symptoms into their seventies and eighties, told *Newsweek* that "frankly, we were somewhat surprised at the magnitude. These traces get seared into the brain and can last a lifetime."

Too embarrassed to seek help until the more populous Vietnam veterans brought their disorder into public consciousness, these aging veterans still "don't always come voluntarily," *Newsweek* reported. "Their wives, who may have been taking the brunt of their erratic behavior, are often the ones to seek help for them." Even their wives had difficulty making the connection between domestic battery and war experience, until women coming out of "the Vietnam era" formed a movement and raised the bar for acceptable male behavior. "I don't know why it took so long," said one woman, who brought her husband into therapy twenty-five years after she'd watched him destroy a hamburger place when a group of high-spirited teenagers accidentally sprayed him with water. "I guess we all had to soldier on," she said. "It was part of that period."

The older we become, the more life experience we acquire, the deeper the recognition of losses and wounds. Twenty years after coming home, Diane Evans was sitting in the sunny bleachers of a tennis court watching her eighteen-year-old son play. She saw beauty itself, and felt the lumpy throat every mother has when a child stirs her gratitude and pride. As the lump rose she felt the familiar, painful swell of love, then she suddenly erupted into uncontrollable sobs. Beauty melted into horror: "There was this boy, my son, lying on a hospital bed with his face blown all to bits."

These scenes are so far removed from the aerial view of war, death so far outside the consciousness of those who contemplate it from a computer screen, the American pilot who accidentally bombed a caravan of his own comrades during Operation Desert Storm was still unable to grasp reality when *60 Minutes* investigated the tragedy months later. America suffered few casualties during the Gulf War, aside from the friendly fire we inflicted on ourselves. The investigation into who was responsible initiated a competitive round of the popular Washington game "It Wasn't Me," as the pilot and the ground commander each tried to persuade Steve Kroft the other was at fault. The question was to be settled when *60 Minutes*, having obtained a recording of their actual dialogue before the bomb was dropped, surprised the pilot by airing the tape.

As the crackling voices between ground and air synchronized data on location and altitude, viewers watched images recreating the virtual reality the pilot saw inside the plane. A fuzzy black-and-white line of straggling troops came into the target sight high above them, the only sign of life in an open sea of sand. Nothing about the flat line below, the strung-out soldiers marching in uneven formation, appeared to be "asking for it." As the pilot centered his aim and waited for a go-ahead it was a horrific moment for viewers, knowing as he had not that the anonymous troops about to be killed were our own. The order came, the trigger was pressed, and as the bomb descended the last words of the pilot broke through the static and cheerfully announced: "This Bud's for you."

The screen exploded with black-and-white bits of vans and wheels and men, then the camera returned to the two men seated in a studio. The heads began talking again, but I remained stuck on those last words. *This Bud's for you?* Have we moved so far from reality that when we're issuing death—whether to our own beloved or the beloved in other countries—we're thinking in *marketing slogans?* I had missed a few seconds of the dialogue, but when I tuned back in Steve Kroft was pursuing his former line of questions. There had apparently been no discussion of how we became a "lite-war" country, nor would there be. The segment was clearly in its final stages: the pilot was subdued, moist around the eyes, barely audible; Steve was grave but triumphant, about to call the match.

So headquarters gave the orders, he said. "It wasn't your fault?"

No, the pilot said. It wasn't his fault.

Thanks to military morale, by 1995 nearly everyone had learned to communicate with bomb-o-grams. The Soviet Union was leveling villages in Chechnya, the French government had resumed testing nuclear bombs, and civilian militias all over the country were now stockpiling arms and loading their trunks with high explosives. Maybe Timothy McVeigh and the other angry young veterans in America today would have found some other path to violence if they hadn't been trained by the army, especially in a culture that offered eighteen thousand televised examples throughout their formative years. But it had to have been a strong shove in that direction at age seventeen to have been taught by your elders that if you've got a problem, go shoot it. So too with the domestic War on Drugs, War on Poverty. When a hammer is the only tool you know how to use, as the familiar adage suggests, you see the whole world as a nail. If your tool is a gun, the whole world becomes a target.

In a culture where marketing slogans and public relations routinely replaced the truth—and without truth there could be no understanding, and therefore no peace—I approached every assignment with a sense of doom. Becoming ever more strident and hysterical, I couldn't turn down the volume in my prose. How could a pilot, even suffering altitude sickness at ten thousand feet, ever mistake a beer for a bomb? Before my circuits blew completely, I mailed my last piece of writing from the drop box on 104th Street—Estaban was right, of course. The editors of the *Women's Review of Books* had asked a half-dozen writers to supply "short, punchy answers" to their annual questionnaire. This was my frantic reply:

1. My morning paper of choice is/used to be ———— *because* ————

I used to read the *New York Times* every day because that's what most of my friends and neighbors read, and I thought I needed to know the same things they did. It was always a trial to get through "the newspaper of record," but ever since the Contract guys took over the front pages it's become unbearable. You can go a dozen pages these days before encountering any news or photos that aren't about the activities of powerful white men. Even when women do appear on the front pages, as corpses or funeral mourners in one of the forty-four wars around the world, the accompanying stories have mainly to do with the activities of men. Last week, I got all the way to the obituary pages and there *still* weren't any headlines or photographs featuring prominent women—we appeared in the fine print below as "cherished mothers" and "beloved wives" and "devoted friends." Since our lives are nearly invisible, it probably shouldn't surprise me that our deaths go unnoticed. I am still looking for a replacement paper, one worthy of the media's alleged "liberal bias."

2. My news organ of choice is —— because ——

I will no doubt return to my habit of scanning two to three dailies every morning, but in the meantime I have a reliable cadre of friends who are compulsive clippers and copiers, and I can depend on them to send me important news by fax. They invariably clue me in to whatever the public-relations teams for O. J. or Newt or the Knicks or the New York Police Department want me to know. What I find genuinely astonishing is that you can skip a whole week of news—despite all the furious, violent, highly publicized outrages—and nothing much has changed. Our "world leaders" remind me of processionary caterpillars, winding us around and around the same rutted track.

3. The funniest/best time I've ever had in the past six months was ——

I have had *many* funny experiences in the last six months during my book tour, although most of the comedy has been inadvertent. I now understand why most of the people who appear on talk shows seem to be on drugs. During a "pre-interview" in a green room in New Jersey, a young producer named Brad was concerned that my slow, midwestern speech lacked the necessary "TV energy." I thought Brad was joking about "TV energy," but he wasn't. He advised me to punch up my inflections, gesture with more feeling. "Oh, I know what you mean, Brad!" I said, getting pretty worked up. "You want me to act more *excited* about almost *everything* than I really *am!*"

"Yes, now you've got it," he said soberly, checking off something on his clipboard. Clearly, Brad didn't get it.

4. *What I most need to escape from these days is* ——*The way I escape/would like to escape is* ——

I need to escape from the results of opinion polls for the next eighteen months, because I know they will tell me that most Americans want prayer in public schools, want Bob Dole to be president, don't want gays in the military, don't want a single-payer health plan. Ever since Ronald Reagan was elected by "an overwhelming majority," I have found myself on the fringes of opinion polls.

I don't know how to escape the feeling of marginality, but I keep thinking about the survival strategy I heard on an answering machine four years ago, when I dialed a wrong number in Ann Arbor, Michigan: "Hi, you've reached Pam and Jane. Please leave your name, your number, and your recommendation for where we should all move if Pat Robertson is elected president." I would call Pam and Jane for their suggestions now, of course, but I don't know their number.

5. *I'm not reading (title, author) these days because* —— (The Bell Curve *and* I Want to Tell You *are assumed on the list. What else? Limit yourself to one book/magazine*).

I'm not reading Robert McNamara these days because I can't bear apologies that take twenty-five years to make. And if George Bush writes about his brave public resignation from the NRA—now that he's no longer dependent on those hefty campaign contributions—I won't read that book either. Talk about profiles in courage. Both are examples of Erik Erikson's theory that most men don't achieve "generativity"—recognition of their responsibility to the next generation—until after they retire. Erikson generously assigned this costly moral delay to the slowness of human development. The darker view is that conscience breaks through only after all power is spent.

6. Any questions you think we should have asked, or reflection you'd like to make:

I'd like to send a wish to the women who will be going to Beijing in September. I know you will have to argue about agendas and priorities and cultural differences and, no doubt, cramped accommodations and slender amenities; I know that some of you will be jet-lagged, stricken with indigestion, suffering insomnia and irregularity; I know, too, how invisible your hard work is to each other, thanks to the boys who run the newspapers and television broadcasts in every nation. Still: Find our common ground, our mutual passion for peace and economic justice. It's clear from the U.N. Report on the Status of Women in 1980—"women constitute half the world's population, perform nearly two-thirds of its work hours, receive one-tenth of the world's income, and own less than one hundredth of the world's property"—that we are exploited but not powerless. Without our bodies and labor, men would have much less money and power to destroy civilizations everywhere. Given the forty-four wars going on around the world, the deadly pace of men's moral development, and the 3.5 million members of the NRA who haven't yet resigned, please don't rule out Lysistrata's strategy without a more effective plan.

IV

The Conquest Mentality Comes Home

THOUGH ARMED CONFLICT appears to have become the major international activity today, most women still tend to be unenthusiastic about war. It offers us fewer starring roles, for one thing. We rarely wield the big weapons or aim the missiles or fly the bomber planes—we still mainly type, nurse, transport, provide intelligence, and dodge bullets. Despite greater enlistments from women in recent years, war remains largely a man's game. We usually play the extras in these spectacular extravaganzas, our legions too numerous and our labor too workaday to be mentioned in the credits.

Even when our role is heroic it's never fun, and rarely noticed. Congress engaged in months of contentious debate over how to memorialize the Vietnam War—conceived by hallucinating madmen and fought by children, it would be embarrassing to have a permanent fixture in Washington that glorified one of the greatest disgraces in U.S. history. It had to be a sober reminder of our reality.

The first installation was Maya Ying Lin's reflective black marble wall, powerful in its stark simplicity, a participatory monument that moves visitors along a grounded view of the accumulated losses. It mourned the casualties of war, but didn't represent of all the wounded survivors. A second monument by sculptor Frederick Hart was added, a bronze statue of three battle-weary soldiers that more closely approximated the traditional homage paid to men who risked their lives. It meant to satisfy the Vietnam veterans who never received a homecoming celebration. But we still didn't have the whole picture.

Women were disappeared from public recognition until Diane Evans and other Vietnam nurses organized a national movement to add a third sculpture, honoring the 265,000 women who served. Dedicated twenty years later on Veteran's Day in 1993, the newest statuary by Glenna Goodacre finally made the courage and sacrifices of the rescuers visible. Still missing, however, is a fourth monument that would acknowledge another group who participated, if we could ever organize our masses. Mothers and wives and lovers were crucial to this war: we supplied the children, arranged the funerals, made the psychiatric appointments, waited for the MIAs and POWs, cleaned up the wreckage in hamburger joints and living rooms, wept at the waste, waste, waste. Every time I visit the Vietnam Memorial I imagine a bronze figure of the Universal Bystander, a lone woman off to the side, facing the Capitol and shaking her fist.

One of the great ironies of war is that propagandists invariably declare the most compelling reason for needing "a strong military"—which means everybody else has to have one, too—is to "protect our women and children." Please. Unarmed civilians accounted for "74 percent of those who died in the wars of the 1980s," Richard J. Barnet reported in *Harper's*. "This figure rose to roughly 90 percent in 1990." If the main purpose of strong militaries is protecting women and children, given the three marines on Okinawa, the officers at Tailhook, the administration at the Citadel, I'm willing to risk whatever the alternative might be.

Whether the fighting takes place on foreign or domestic soil, the violence of every war eventually comes home. As our military protection currently stands, American women are having much more trouble defending ourselves from domestic men in uniform. In yet another replay of the Tailhook drama, at a recent convention of the NYPD in Washington, D.C., several dozen drunken boys shed their blues—except for their gunbelts—and ran naked through hotel corridors, spraying beer on the carpets and bullets into the ceilings, bullying and harassing female guests until in desperation the hotel called . . . whom? The police? The navy? The marines?

When the Joint Chiefs insist on the superior virtue of military morale I have to suppose they don't know most of the facts in the box, though many have been in the public domain for years. In the canons of military morale, sex and death have been inseparably connected—although history textbooks, like the *New York Times*, are reluctant to discuss this connection at any length. During World War II, 5 million copies of Rita Hayworth's sensuous pose in *Life* were circulated among American troops, one of which was pasted to the nose of "the first nuclear weapon detonated over Bikini atoll in 1946," author Susan Griffin reports in *A Chorus of Stones*. This phallic association with bombs continues today, as newspapers have confirmed rumors that the pilots of Operation Desert Storm were pumped up for their bombing missions with pornography films supplied by the army.

The merger of sex and death is not unique to American troops, of course. Reporting to headquarters after exploding two Cessnas and killing four Brothers to the Rescue, the

Cuban pilot who fired the missiles "gleefully spoke of shooting off his targets 'cojones,'" according to *Time* magazine. The Japanese government, so distressed by the crimes of foreign aggressors, announced that it will pay restitution to the surviving Korean and peasant women kidnapped during World War II to "staff" their own army's "comfort stations." And by now Susan Brownmiller and others have documented, in harrowing detail, how the German army raped Jews, the British army raped Bangladeshi, the French army raped Algerians. How are we to be shocked by the everyday stuff of the Serbian army? The Serbian "penetration" orders simply institutionalized what every other army had been doing haphazardly throughout history. Can anyone believe that the persistent, haunting memories of our own Vietnam veterans, still having so much trouble reentering domestic reality, have nothing to do with rape?

Despite all this evidence, the Chiefs are apparently unaware that some reverberation of military morale is rippling through the body politic even as they speak: Every 18 seconds, a woman beaten; every two and a half minutes, one of us raped. Do they imagine we "wanted it"? If the Chiefs do most of their serious thinking in rooms with no view, facing reflections of their own beribboned images, do they even know we are out here, witnessing this ludicrous virtue in action?

Thinking about military morale makes anyone without a damping apparatus long for the entire contents of Hunter Thompson's trunk. Otherwise, it's impossible to go right past the phrase "his penis was cut" without putting some meaning back into those words—making them whole, disarming their power to hurt us. To analyze the whole of military morale—which brought us not only the Chiefs' sexual-identity crisis, but also the radioactive wastes in the Arctic, the megadeficits in world economies, the lust for nuclear weapons in "developing countries," the wars and cleansings and shootings and killings around the globe—it's necessary to look at how the body politic got enmeshed in the Cold War, a consentual reality in which it was considered a sane activity to plan the destruction of whole civilizations. To unravel an absurdity of this magnitude means probing our political formative years, forty years ago when the Superpowers were only babies.

After the widely reported atrocities of World War II sent shock waves around the globe, international leaders faced the sobering task of rebuilding Western civilization. "Let us be alert." Viktor Frankl implored from the mental-health capital of the world in 1946. "Since Auschwitz we know what man is capable of. And since Hiroshima we know what is at stake." Especially in the United States—a young, rich, energetic country least damaged by the war—politicians faced an identity crisis: Who should we be this time? What kind of competition should we set up with Russia for the coveted title of Number One—Intellectual? Athletic? Economic? Military? What would be the surest means of persuading Russia not to take advantage of us—and would we ever want to take some advantage of them? What kind of reality, as Frank Oppenheimer might have asked, did we want to make up?

Once more, a brilliant seer appeared fortuitously to remind us that personal sanity depended on the mental health of our political systems: "War makes less and less rational, practical sense as an instrument of long-term national self-interest," Walter Lippmann wrote in *The Good Society*, pointing out that "war tears apart huge populations which have become dependent upon one another for their standard of life—in some degree, for life itself." Since World War II was clearly suicidal to everyone involved—the Japanese kamikaze pilots being only the most extreme example of soldiers following death orders—Lippmann felt the future depended on creating "a wholly new orientation of the human race."

According to UC-Berkeley professor Robert Bellah and four colleagues who coauthored *The Good Society*—a kind of socioanalysis of our national depression—Walter Lippmann was a pragmatist, not a dreamer. He argued the *rationality* of using global equity as our primary defense strategy: Fairness and compassion were not only the most dependable routes to world stability and lasting peace, but also far easier on the psyches of citizens drafted to carry them out. For the sake of survival and sanity, Lippmann urged us to widen democratic participation inside and outside national borders; create economic systems accountable to public interests first, profit interests second; keep the goods of every society balanced and sufficient to counteract predatory nations; and recognize that however we, a Superpower, defined our values and exercised our strength, so goes the developing world.

It's hard not to weep, thinking about how newspapers today might read had we chosen the virtual reality of the Good Society. Instead of shell-shocked soldiers haunted by experiences of violence, our Vietnam veterans would have come home with practice in compassion. The military-industrial complex would be churning out food, clothing, medicine, Plymouths, and Cuisinarts to keep the good life balanced around the world. The CIA would be commissioned to infiltrate countries experiencing unrest with plans for parks and recreation centers. If being the world's Number One Friend had become our national identity forty years ago, the whole concept of "global warming" would have a different . . . but stop. Come back to reality. We did not choose Walter Lippmann's plan.

The Good Society had one fatal psychological flaw—it was too far ahead on the learning curve for Superpowers still in their childhood. The U.S. was then a bullish young country, a teenager with a hydrogen bomb. Becoming a mature society required what psychiatrists call "delayed gratification"—a thoughtful, responsible approach to managing the omnipresent temptations of the pleasure principle. The political leaders of our country instead succumbed to the need for immediate gratification, promising chickens in every pot, cars in every driveway, mortgages for every home. "It is a characteristic of the American culture that, again and again, one is commanded and ordered to 'be happy,'" Frankl observed from Vienna. He noted again that "one must have a reason to 'be happy.' Once that reason is found, however, one becomes happy automatically."

Certainly, the temptations to pursue happiness rather than meaning were enormous for the baby Superpowers—greater by far than for any other generation in history. With the mushroom cloud in everyone's face, American capitalists could take all the stuff they wanted from weaker countries—rubber, copper, gold, diamonds, minerals, oil—and get it cheap. With our strong military supporting dictators willing to exploit their own people, we suppressed any "global unrest" caused by our methods of doing business. We teamed up with neighborhood bullies like Manuel Noriega and rewarded them with the goods they most coveted: weapons.

We became the world's largest exporter of arms, and by 1991, our burgeoning munitions industry was profiting more than $23 billion worldwide. Marketing wasn't a problem, since we offered continual reminders of what arms can do: we blew things up now and then: pointed missiles at Cuba; invaded Vietnam, Cambodia, Libya, Grenada, Nicaragua, the Panama Canal, wherever. After our neighbors were convinced we were dangerous enough, we could do anything.

The bewildered herd, busy with mortgage payments

and raising large families, weren't thinking ahead about what it could mean to support an economy dependent on exporting death, if they made the connection between our Dow Jones averages and world news at all. Maybe the bystander culture thought "arms production" meant hunting rifles. In reality, we were exporting enough chemicals and hardware to wipe out Manhattan and irradiate New England for thousands of years, if just one little bunch of the thugs in our gang got really pissed off about something. In Somalia alone, U.S. suppliers had sold enough guns for the entire population to kill itself five times. As an anonymous Pentagon official told the *New York Times*, "between the stuff the Russians and we stuck in there during the great Cold War, there are enough arms in Somalia to fuel hostility for 100 years."

It is grotesque that the Cold War is so often celebrated as a 'long peace' maintained by nuclear deterrence," Richard Barnet wrote. "The so-called peace unfolded against a background of mass slaughter of Asians, Africans, and Latin Americans, all by non-nuclear weapons. During the Cold War years, at least 20 million people died in more than 120 wars. Most Americans still do not have any idea of the dimensions of the slaughter of Guatemala and El Salvador," or of the ethnic cleansings accomplished worldwide with U.S. weapons. Mark Danner reported in the *New Yorker* that Honduran soldiers conquering the village of El Mozote threw babies in the air and caught them on bayonets, made in the USA. What kind of films do armies supply to pump troops up for that kind of combat?

While the Superpowers may certainly take credit for curbing world population growth with 120 wars, the women survivors who made it to Beijing were unanimous in their preference for diaphragms. The same Christian fundamentalists who supported the sale of death machines to Middle-Eastern and Central American regimes during

Reagan's administration simultaneously opposed, on moral grounds, UNICEF's plan to distribute free birth-control supplies during its global immunization program. For the first time in history, doctors and nurses would be making simultaneous house calls on every mother and child around the world, some traveling by camel with refrigerated trunks, some landing on rural airstrips lighted by candles—a monumental achievement, requiring international cooperation and philanthropy. During the planning stage, when these humanitarian Albert Schweitzers around the world recognized a historic opportunity, they expanded their goal to provide women everywhere with safe birth control. They were stunned when our actor president aborted the plan by threatening to withdraw U.S. funds. From suffering locales in missionary hospitals and rural clinics, medical professionals around the world couldn't see the sense in the American fundamentalist position: If women didn't keep reproducing children to be conscripted and targeted in war, who was going to need all our bombs? A Muslim doctor from South Africa who grew up with war asked me why sensible Americans kept letting the nitwits among us do so much damage. I shook my head, told her you'd really have to live here to see how diaphragms came to be a threat to national security.

Some four decades into the Cold War, when it finally dawned on the bewildered that selling missiles and weapons to despots and drug dealers might not be a terrific idea, a frantic effort was made to create an impenetrable shield around the country. In 1983, we embarked on the $30-billion "Star Wars" program. While this virtual reality drew the line for how much fantasy most of the media would swallow, Pentagon officials impressed a credulous Congress with mountainous data and videotapes documenting phenomenal success. In one tape, legislators watched a test where our new heat-seeking missile exploded a prototype enemy missile in mid-flight—well, not an *exact* prototype. Congress didn't learn until 1993 that the target missile had been outfitted with artificial heating devices that made it ten times more vulnerable to the interceptor, as well as with outside explosives in case "we just happened to nip it," as General Eugene Fox explained. For our minuteman missile searching the sky, the enemy was a redcoat beating a drum.

"The debate now is not whether the test was rigged, but how it was rigged," the *Times* reported during the 1993 hearing. "A former Reagan Administration official, a nuclear physicist who closely studied the missile-defense program," said that "it was characterized by secrecy, greed, self-deception, deception of the Congress and actually even of the President." For $30 billion, the Star Wars program gave us a few science-fiction videotapes and a ton of paper lies, but its defenders still claim success, saying it hastened the collapse of the Soviet Union "by accelerating Soviet defense spending and thus damaging the Soviet economy." Not to mention ours. Had we not thrown billions of dollars out the window on Pentagon power dreams and spent them on education and health care and road repairs—or even more $1000 executive toilet seats—there would be far less depression and irregularity today. As it is, comprehending the superiority of military morale becomes more of a challenge every day. The latest Pentagon disinformation campaign is barely unraveled before the next CIA scandal starts competing for space on the front page.

Since nothing becomes reality without our consent, the Cold War could never have happened unless our leaders first persuaded us to go along with the concept of mass incineration. The human longing for love, peace, meaning were stubborn psychological desires to reprogram in the body politic. Often squeamish about bloodshed and suffering, we Americans had to learn to live with daily threats of violence to ourselves and be willing to follow up on threats to others. We had to block out knowledge of the past and live as through there were no tomorrow. This was a colossal psychological task—especially since postwar parents were raising the greatest number of children in American history.

Rather than widening participation, as Lippmann proposed, secrecy and denial became the guiding philosophy of the Cold War. As the slogan on the caps the CIA distributed to the Nicaraguan contras summarized it: "ADMIT NOTHING—DENY EVERYTHING—MAKE COUNTER ACCUSATIONS." This principle, in order to work for the military, had to seep into every institution connected with it—the media, the business community, organized religions, higher education, even the institution of marriage—before the consentual reality of the Cold War could come true. Big job, converting a civilization.

A besieged postwar media, inundated with news from around the world, became an immediate ally to military morale. Then as now, an obedient press corps would attend staged conferences and "write down the words of powerful people, who frequently lied," then "print the words and have its columnists double-dome them," Molly Ivins observed. Reporters and editors fell into the habit of quoting military language directly, without supplying the necessary translations of army-speak about what the Department of Defense was actually doing. Or why.

It would be three long decades before the Freedom of Information Act opened government files and allowed Professor Noam Chomsky, the distinguished linguist at MIT, and other researchers to inform us that when the Department of Defense spoke about "defending free trade," it actually meant threatening weaker countries who wouldn't surrender their goods to our capitalists; "collateral damage" meant dead civilians; "surgical strikes" meant the bombing of shoe factories; "strategic deterrence" meant planning and building and hiding massive arsenals of nuclear weapons. "Allocations for a strong military" meant spending trillions of dollars we didn't have on weapons we hoped never to use.

With a sanitized vocabulary to dull objections from the squeamish and frequent invocations of "democracy and freedom" ringing in our ears, we were encouraged to think of ourselves as the Good Society even while entering the opposite reality with the Soviet Union: we embarked on MAD, "Mutually Assured Destruction." As Professor Carol Cohn, working at the Center for Psychological Studies in the Nuclear Age at Harvard University Medical School, pointed out in "Sex and Death in the Rational World of Defense Intellectuals," the sterility and secrecy of military language spared good men from having to think about the effects "clean bombs" could have on women and children and vegetable gardens. In fact, Cold War language made it impossible to hold any concept of human life in mind. It was "purged of feeling, disembodied, uttered as if by no one with an earthly existence," Susan Griffin wrote. After the meaning dropped out of military language, civilians trying to know the truth heard only "Blah, blah, blah."

"What is hidden, kept secret, cannot be lived," Griffin noted. "It exists in a place of exile, outside the realm of response." She wondered how the sign posted at Wendover Air Base, where pilots trained for their historic mission over Hiroshima, influenced family lives: "WHAT YOU HEAR HERE, WHAT YOU SEE HERE, WHEN YOU LEAVE HERE, LET IT STAY HERE." She imagined Laura Fermi living in a "chasm of speechlessness" with her husband, Enrico, unable to offer a toast at the party they hosted when the first nuclear chain reaction was successfully tested at Los Alamos. She didn't know, couldn't know, what they were celebrating.

Without words, without meaning, the virtual reality of

the Cold War seeped into the personal relationships of men and women, fathers and mothers, the psyches of young children. The Baby Boom generation was permanently imprinted by the image of the mushroom cloud. Secret decisions made in Washington had a direct impact on my kindergarten finger painting two thousand miles away, as air-raid sirens drilled terror into my head. A popular consentual reality in the fifties was that because we had agreed to a peace strategy of Mutually Assured Destruction, small children should be trained to duck and take cover under their desks during hydrogen explosions. The Baby Boomers spent their school years crouched down between the wooden runners, ears pounding, minds squeezing with dread that this could be IT.

The mushroom cloud provides a riveting clue to the aetiology of my generation, which later latched onto the runners of corporate ladders with a frenzied, irresponsible compulsion to "eat, drink and be merry, for tomorrow . . ." Indulging the need for immediate gratification to historic excess, we entered the job market guided by the slogan appearing on T-shirts in the eighties: "WHOEVER DIES WITH THE MOST TOYS WINS." Reversing Lippmann's theory for a better tomorrow—public interest first, private interest next—we plundered Wall Street with merger mania, created vast unemployment with hostile takeovers, polluted the environment with deregulation. Again, these unrealities were accomplished under such amorphous explanations as "market forces . . . supply and demand . . . economic competitiveness," as though our mortal economic arrangements were acts of God or scientific laws, unshaped by human will.

Perhaps the "chasm of speechlessness" that began with the Fermis and lingers so provocatively today can be traced to this longtime habit of secrecy and denial. Author Deborah Tannen outlines the many difficulties women and men are having revealing their feelings in *You Just Don't Understand*, and in "Tangled and Dark" songwriter Bonnie Raitt croons for us all to get "Way on into it, baby, down where your feelings are parked." But what if this current communication disorder is not an inability to express our feelings—what if it's that we can't talk about what we're doing? Every day there are stories, reported and not, of sexual harassment, race discrimination, pay inequity, social injustice. What if our speechlessness is in fact another symptom of our political depression, a silent testimony that our work, our lives, have to be "purged of feeling" to carry on? "If you talked about it," as Joan Furey had said, "you couldn't do your job." If young men had thought about it, for example, how could the Serbian soldiers follow orders to rape the enemy?

According to the newspapers, some of the soldiers apologized before carrying out their orders—assuring Muslim women they meant nothing personal. But can a soldier, even under orders, produce an erection without engaging his own mind? Does he think about his wife—bring a loved one into the scene? Or do screams of terror provoke other images, perhaps from a film his army provided? When the soldier comes home, is he able to keep the women he loves separate from the enemies he violated so intimately—or do they merge, all women now capable of stimulating cruel memories, guilt, self-hatred, repugnance, violence? Does the soldier's young wife, hearing his nightmares, ask what happened on the front? Does he tell her? A fact this size— sixty thousand rapes—cannot be carried out anonymously. Told or untold, such facts become excruciatingly personal.

It's no wonder we break out in a cold sweat reading the newspapers. The virtual realities we have been living in for the last forty years not only split the atom, but severed men from their wives, children from their parents, people from their feelings, and meaning from our work. Again, the virtual reality we thought we had nothing to do with has infected every fiber of our beings, every tendril of our psyches. Turning the pages, we encounter daily evidence of world violence, tragic economies, brutal business practices, damage to our oceans, forests, vegetable gardens, even our personal relationships. How we talk. What we do in bed.

. . . ONE NATION UNDER
GOD, INDIVISIBLE . . .

◆

PART THREE

Sustaining the Gaze

V

Talking Heads and Hostess Twinkies

"I LIKE TO think that all things are true, but only partly true, in dialectical fashion, more true than what came before, less true than what comes after," my brother Frank wrote in his last letter to me fifteen years ago. "Even Adolf Hitler was in at least one way better than the Weimar Republic, moving from the concept of a kingdom ruled by autocratic powers to the concept of the Deutsch Volk, the living organic unity, however monstrous and terrible was the war and the concentration camps. I have to believe that if I believe God is good. The reason we have suffering is that progress can only be achieved at a price, because goodness has to be made out of badness, and the raw material has to be refined by fire and mixed with alloys before it can become strong. This is what I like to believe, anyway. The alternative is to believe that we are subject to invasions of absurdity and chaos for no reason at all."

Even when he wasn't in a manic phase of his illness, Frank was a passionate debater. He wore opponents down by reciting chapter and verse from Kafka's *Trial* or St. Paul's Letter to the Ephesians or Mike Royko's latest column in the *Chicago Daily News*. A voracious reader stuck with nearly total recall, he spent his life trying to integrate Catholic theology with Freudian psychology, Søren Kierkegaard with D. T. Suzuki, Karl Marx with Adam Smith, trying to make all the partial truths he'd acquired come into some kind of unified whole. Incapable of small talk at weddings and graduations, he usually sat next to Grandma Manney, who under family pressure had cheerfully succumbed to wearing a hearing aid, but rarely turned it on. Frank's employers and seminary advisors often mistook his insatiable curiosity for insubordination or heresy. Long past childhood, he was still under siege from the question he could never satisfy: But *why?*

During our last visit in Fort Wayne, it struck me in the middle of one of our marathon talks that we weren't really conversing. I nodded every now and then, while he continuously unloaded. He appeared lighter as he boarded the Greyhound, and I remember worrying through his elated, manic good-bye that he was headed into another terrifying high, when reason abandoned him altogether and he floated to the far reaches of madness. It was impossible to argue him down again, and frankly, it made me lose heart to try. The undiluted joy he found out there beyond reason seemed to me the only time he was truly happy, unburdened by the facts. How could I plead with an exuberant man in love with God, in love with *you*, to please quit the histrionics and come back to reality?

Since my family history was riddled with episodes of "nervous breakdowns," and my own personal history contained some rather colossal departures from reality, I committed myself quite voluntarily last June to solitary confinement in this little cabin on the shore of Crooked Lake in upper Michigan, just above the forty-fifth parallel.

When I'd driven past the sign marking the latitude on Route 31, "Halfway to the North Pole," I remember thinking: Why go halfway? In my state of despond four months ago, the North Pole sounded like it had my name on it. I imagined starting a new life, maybe opening an espresso stand. How many cappuccinos would the six customers I might find there have to order per day for me to break even? Air-freight expenses for supplies would be hefty—given the activities of the Superpowers for the last half century, the water supply wasn't safe even at the North Pole. Certainly, I would not take the toxic Blue Box with me. I would just leave it in the Ladies Room at the next service station . . .

Instead, I obediently followed the directions I had been given and pulled into the long driveway next to the wet-lands. I had neither Frank's nerve nor his craziness. I turned off the Rabbit and then sat, keys in my lap, staring through the windshield for a few minutes, or maybe a few hours. The world-weary journalist in Penelope Lively's novel *Moon Tiger*, writing from the trenches of World War II, despairs that she will ever comprehend the whole truth: "Because I cannot shed my skin and put on yours, cannot strip my mind of its knowledge and its prejudices, cannot look cleanly at the world with the eyes of a child, I am as imprisoned by my time as you were by yours." My brother found relief from the existential sorrow of "invasions of absurdity and chaos for no reason at all" by depositing his considerable faith in God. Rather than shaking this belief, his madness solidified it. My route out of depression required me to stick with the partly true facts, thinking and rethinking until I could assemble some kind of logical whole. Without faith, I had to find meaning in absurdity.

I didn't open the Blue Box for the first few weeks. My shock-receiving capacity was still in the shop, as it were, and the urge to write all but nonexistent. I spent those days walking the dunes along Lake Michigan, scanning the horizon and priming my goosebump receptor. Without it, there was no chance I'd be able to see the whole picture. My capacity for joy seemed to have atrophied, since it hadn't been exercised much by the news.

I would watch the vacationing families on the beach, think about my own, observe how beautiful love looks in the eyes, the faces, the gestures of human beings. Stripped down to their essential selves, without power suits and briefcases and Day Runner appointment books, people on beaches looked like endangered species in a protected environment. Here, you see so much more goodness than badness. Of course, this was a privileged middle-class population I was observing—you need enough money to remove yourself and your loved ones from civilization for a spell, to catch your breath and repair relationships. When former Michigan governor James Blanchard appointed Dr. Agnes Mansour, a Sister of Mercy, to his cabinet as Director of Social Services, she traveled around the state explaining to taxpayers that the poor need "food, clothing, shelter, and rest." Poverty is exhausting, she said. No one could get their life back on track without rest. If Agnes Mansour and the Sisters of Mercy had drafted our welfare-reform legislation, we'd now be debating how much to spend on vacations for welfare mothers.

Maybe Congress should adjourn to the beach to weigh their important deliberations on who should get what and how much. The Michigan parents strolling the shore with small children seemed to take a benevolent approach to their socializing responsibilities, finding mutual pleasure in dispensing hot dogs and ice cream instead of the usual "Just Say No" often elicited under home pressures. Perhaps Archbishop Desmond Tutu had observed this magnanimity at South Africa's beaches in 1989 when he proposed a peaceful demonstration at the Strand, a whites-only beach on the Indian Ocean outside Cape Town. How could white parents enjoying children frolicking in the waves prohibit black parents and children from doing the same?

By the time the black families arrived, however, the view of the horizon was already blocked. A row of police, their backs to the sea, greeted the new arrivals with loaded guns and barking dogs. In the virtual reality of apartheid, it was their bizarre job to keep black people out of the ocean. Had any of the men in the firing line that day chanced to turn around for a moment, looked away from their black-and-white job on the shore and into the radiant blues of the South African horizon, they might have asked the humbling questions such vastness provokes: Who am I? What am I doing here? Where do I, a mere integer, fit into the flow chart of the universe? Had the uniformed men holding the beach gotten even a glimpse of this larger reality, they could never have unleashed the dogs and gunfire that maimed their own people that day.

My friend Zubeida Jaffers, a journalist and activist during the South African anti-apartheid movement, attended the Strand demonstration with her three-year-old daughter Ruschka. Excited by the waves and not comprehending the meaning of the police line, Ruschka started making a beeline for the water. Catching her hand and pulling her back to a safe distance, Zubeida had to tell her she couldn't go swimming that day. Couldn't, in fact, even dip her toes in the water. Ruschka vented the immense frustration that thwarted toddlers are famous for around the globe, then asked, "But Mommy, *why?*"

How to explain the concept of apartheid to a child? How to tell her the truth for her own safety, without damaging her growing self-esteem? What to say when the facts elicited even more anguished whys? "Ruschka," Zubeida said softly, "you cannot swim on this beach because you are not white." Ruschka looked down at her tummy and frowned, thinking this over. She knew the names of colors by then but hadn't gotten to racism yet. She lifted the edge of her alabaster sweater and said, "But Mommy, I *am* white today."

I wasn't the only dreamer who came to the beach to get away from it all only to discover I still had most of it with me. As I walked the shore of Lake Michigan, two women absorbed in an intense conversation approached from the opposite direction. From their expressions, I'd assumed they were exchanging indignation over a demented boss or oblivious spouse. It turned out to be a case of indigestion over the Sunday news.

"He's not just a lunatic—he's a lunatic with guns!" one said.

"Don't forget God and guts," her friend dryly noted.

They were talking about Norm Olsen, the leader of the Michigan Militia, headquartered a few miles from the Petoskey State Beach. There was no shortage of Norms in the heartland—the Michigan Militia was comprised of an estimated fifteen thousand men with guns and bad attitudes. People registered shock, but it was hardly a surprise to find huge pockets of undisciplined rage across America. Our public rhetoric and hate radio have been cultivating these troops for the past fifteen years. The vigilantes in Michigan—and the forty-four citizen militia identified in other states after the Oklahoma City bombing—are the predictable outcome of the social irresponsibility we've been trying to ignore, dismiss, tolerate for decades. The $23 billion earned annually by our munitions industry had not only supplied weapons for the civil war in Somalia, of course—hostile vigilantes preparing to secede from the Union were armed to the hilt right here in Michigan.

With fifteen thousand militia men in the neighborhood, it was strange not to see any obvious representatives at the beach. In this place where the world is more beautiful than not, you don't see the same reality as the one presented in the media. Out here where the headlines are lived, human beings seem to share more in common than not: we are not all racists, we are not all violent, we are not all greedy. Then why does it take so long to make the connections between Us and Them? The media, the definers of civilization who decide what's good and what's bad, what matters and what doesn't, has us preoccupied with all the wrong questions. Our thinking factories in newsrooms and television studios, rather than helping us across the terrible divide between Us and Them, have instead institutionalized it.

To keep up with fast-breaking news around the world, "we are compelled to reduce the knowable to a schema," Primo Levi wrote. This formulaic reporting "shuns half-tints and complexities: it is prone to reduce the river of human occurrences to conflicts, and the conflicts to duels— we and they, Athenians and Spartans, Romans and Carthaginians." The conflict construct of the media filters all news through the same questions: who's winning, who's losing; who's advancing, who's retreating; who's embarrassed, who's saving face; who's suing, defending, plea bargaining, or prosecuting whom.

Before I stopped reading the Sunday *New York Times* I used to make lists of the "action verbs" in headlines every week, to see what percentage had to do with conflict and competition. It was a very peaceful week if the conflict between opposing sides—liberals and conservatives, labor and business, pro-life and pro-choice, Christians and humanists—dropped below 75 percent. With the exception of the sports pages, where "defeats" or "stomps" or "trounces" did not inflict injury except to unlucky bettors, we Americans were mainly preoccupied with capturing, demanding, defending, bombing, capitulating, defaulting, breaking, and destroying . . . or so it would seem.

To fit into the conflict schema, every news maker has to

be neatly paired against his or her Antichrist. The ethical obligation for accuracy and fairness in reporting has been reduced to the practice of objectivity, hastily satisfied by "quoting both sides." Which means there have to be sides, given equal space, even if one consists of almost two hundred thousand women with breast implants and the other is a spokesman for the Dow Chemical Company. If you have something important to say, you need to find someone to say the opposite before you can be heard.

When sides aren't available, of course, the media can create one: If there were feminists, there had to be "anti-feminists." Consciously or not, the media has fed the backlash against the women's movement by quoting an "anti" every time a new study was released about wage discrimination or domestic violence, however wacky or irresponsible the opposing argument might be. In the seventies, during the decade-long debate on the Equal Rights Amendment, Joan Uebelhoer and I were often paired off against members of the Eagle Forum. Talk-show producers called them debates, "but what they really want are female cat fights," Joan observed. The local media in Fort Wayne often had a hard time finding an adversary who matched Joan's sharp wit and intelligence. One producer actually called her for suggestions.

"Who do you think is really good from the other side?" he asked.

"Who do I think is *good*?" she asked, incredulous. "Nobody. When you asked Vernon Jordan to come on your show, did you ask him who's good in the Klan?"

Stereotypes became shorthand for complex issues: the press covered the great campaign for women's independence as a Super Bowl between "libbers" and "homemakers." Educating the media while she educated the public, Joan, a former homemaker herself and mother of five, was often exasperated by the rude questions and wild assumptions about feminist "man-haters." Once we were on a local radio show with two opponents who had circulated the rumor we were lesbians, since we had both publicly supported gay rights, and the host appeared visibly shaken at the possibility. Joan and I, however, did not turn out to be his main problem. Eagle Forum debaters had undergone media training that taught them, essentially, to wear peach and take no prisoners.

Employing Phyllis Schlafly's abrasive tactics, they interrupted, ran overtime, and dominated the microphones with a fierceness the addled moderator was unequipped to handle. During the second commercial break, Joan decided to use rumor to our advantage. Just before we came back on the air she looked directly into our most vocal opponent's eyes and said, warmly and softly, "Alice, I think I'm falling in love with you." It worked immediately—Alice was fairly speechless for the remainder of the hour.

The reality "out here" is misrepresented by this conflict construct of the media, since it makes the daily heroism of ordinary people more or less invisible. A feature story will occasionally offer an inspiring account of a courageous teacher or humanitarian philanthropist, but these stories arrive as "soft news," exceptions to the ruling facts in the neighboring headlines. Domestic life is rarely mentioned in the conflict view of national life, unless a wife goes temporarily insane and severs her husband's penis, or a distraught mother, contemplating suicide, instead drowns her children. Then we notice "something's wrong here" . . . too late. Even motherhood is slotted into the Us-and-Them frame: the traditional mother versus the single mother, the middle-class mom versus the welfare mom, as if we did not have much more in common than the differences in our checkbooks.

The stereotypes don't hold up if we happen to meet each other face-to-face. Republican strategist Frank Luntz organizes focus groups to study how to phrase things so middle-class people won't be upset about starving the Other America—a process in which "cutting Medicare" becomes "curbing the growth of Medicare." When he put old people on Social Security at the same table with young people seeking student loans, he found they were much more likely to support each other's needs. To get any punitive campaigns off the ground, it's essential that we see each other as "special interest groups." That is, my advantage must be your disadvantage.

Before legislation debates in 1995, a welfare agency in Washington assigned each of its state senators a personal welfare mother, committing them to a long series of dialogues. Many of the senators were quite shaken by the encounter, as "the poor" they met did not match the media image. One senator said that in subsequent debates it was not unusual for his colleagues to counter an argument, "Well *my* mother said . . ."

It's a shame Indiana didn't yoke its state legislators to reality before they passed the Personal Responsibility Act. They used the Beltway approach in the War on Poverty, looking at the poor through flow charts and computer screens. Persuaded by Governor Evan Bayh's slogan "Paychecks, not welfare checks!" they voted to improve the character of Indiana's recipients of AFDC (Aid to Families with Dependent Children) by putting mothers to work in the fifteen hundred McDonald's across the state: "It's not glamorous, but it's a job," Governor Bayh said, apparently unaware all these women already had jobs.

"This workfare program is just infuriating," said Joan. As Welfare Director of Allen County, she was not looking forward to implementing the new legislation. "Most of the women in my program are not only raising their own kids— they're taking care of other people's too." The working poor—neighbors and relatives who can't afford day care on the current minimum wage—rely on these stay-at-home moms to work for no pay at all. It will cost the state a fortune to replace this vital volunteer labor force, although this may be the one redeeming quality of the Personal Responsibility Act: when Indiana has to hire day-care employees to replace welfare moms working at McDonald's, it could finally establish a minimum wage for motherhood. Joan thought the economics of the reform legislation were half-baked, but the morality was wholly insupportable.

As *Washington Post* columnist Richard Cohen summarized the racism in the media coverage of the poor, "in the popular imagination it is not whites who have children out of wedlock, spend a lifetime on welfare, and shoot themselves up with dope and the neighborhood with lead. It's 'them.'" The Indiana media was so effective in its character assassination of the poor, a middle-class mom catapulted into Joan's office by post-divorce poverty asked her if there were some short forms for temporary welfare cases like herself. She didn't plan to be needy for long—said she was glad, in fact, "that you're finally cracking down on those people."

"*What* people?" Joan asked, inviting the woman to notice her uncanny resemblance to the other applicants in line. The average client in Allen County could fit the profile of Newt Gingrich's former wife: most were mature mothers who had struggled with double shifts for years, raising kids alone on lower-income jobs while better-paid fathers defaulted on child support. "These are the women I now have to ask to sign *personal responsibility* pledges," Joan had said madly. Enraged at the indignities and invasions of privacy she would be required to administer, she resigned.

While the silent majority has a hard time surfacing in any recognizable way in the media, the habit of "respect" for high officeholders—from CEOs to the president to the pope—also inhibits free speech, preventing the press from raising "impertinent questions." Despite hordes of reporters surrounding the pope on his first American visit, it was Theresa Kane, a Sister of Mercy, who had to do their job: she knelt down before the pope, kissed his ring, then asked when he thought women could become "full partners" in the church. This question was becoming ever more critical for American women, inside and outside the church, especially as the Catholic hierarchy became more and more involved in the political issues of abortion, reproduction and sexuality. What follow-up reports did this incident produce? Myriad stories on whether the pope was "embarrassed," whether Sister Kane would be bounced from the Sisters of Mercy, whether the Vatican could control the radical American nuns.

Given the blah, blah, blah that generally passes for commentary, the direct honesty in *Hip Mama*, a "parenting 'zine" published by a group of single young mothers in Berkeley, provided a startling contrast. Under the headline "Ohio Judge Gets a Clue," the magazine reported that Hamilton County judge Albert Mestemaker "ordered a man who pleaded no contest to a domestic violence charge to marry the woman he hit." Reversing the order after it caused a national furor, the judge conceded the ruling was "ill-conceived." With all due respect, *Hip Mama* observed: "No shit, Your Honor."

This kind of forthright honesty is rare in the mainstream media. The *Boston Globe* startled the public when it ran an editorial generally supporting former President Jimmy Carter's anti-inflation program under the astonishing headline "Mush from the Wimp." The joke headline ran in 140,000 papers before it was caught. The embarrassed *Globe* editors publicly apologized for the "inappropriate" headline and said the editorial was supposed to have been called "All Must Share the Burden."

"That's the part that got us," Meg Greenfield wrote in a sympathetic editorial in the *Washington Post*, admitting that her own paper "must have used that headline a thousand times. In fact—or as we Big Thinks like to say, '*Indeed*'—just put us in the presence of that headline and, we can't help ourselves, we start automatically and compulsively writing the editorial that goes with it." Greenfield said that in the end, when "all editorial writers are called to judgment, it won't be the headline pranks run amok, that sort of thing, that will get us. No, it will be all those other miles of editorial prose that fit so nicely under the headline 'All Must Share the Burden' for which we will, collectively, fry. Say this for whoever it was at the *Globe* who did the Mush from the Wimp headline: Somebody over there is alive—no longer employed, perhaps, but alive. And that's already something."

The silent majority has so thoroughly adjusted to the dissembling, it's now fatal for politicians to be truthful with us. Any candidate who admits that capitalism as we know it is not benefiting the majority has about as much chance of being elected as a cardinal who allows that birth control might be a good idea has of becoming the next pope. After decades of failure to question authority, we now have a politics as insubstantial as hair mousse.

Readers and viewers following the news today get the facts, nothing but the facts. The rules of objectivity require those who cover the momentous or tragic events of our day—who might actually have some insight into who's making sense and who's lying—to refrain from telling us what to think. This leaves bystanders, stripped of their innocence, in a state of acute anxiety—especially when the path to activism is unclear. "I do not think it is enough to raise consciousness and 'muster the facts,'" women's studies professor Ellen Morgan wrote. "People go from alienation into activism too often without having an accurate notion of the psychic toll they are paying and will go on paying."

After my Women's Studies students spent a semester raising their consciousness, for example, they didn't like sounding "strident and hysterical" but didn't know what to do about it. After learning to see things differently, they had a hard time living among the unsighted without feeling crazy all the time. At the end of each semester, I would ask my students to take their "alienation temperature"—measure the distance between what they wanted and what they had. This question always produced the most voluminous responses in their journals: they cited arguments with bosses, fights with husbands, minor skirmishes at cocktail parties and bridge tables, painful confrontations with mothers and antifeminist friends. Small group discussions provided a sanity check—they discovered the resistance to their feminism was real and unselective. It was political, not personal. When students detailed the number and scope of the changes that needed to be made, they were able to modify their expectations of one conversation, one week, one year.

Professor Morgan encouraged her students to seek the "psychic rest and pleasure that are necessary to prevent burnout," and reminded them to celebrate small changes in order to "live as feminists in their society, despite its sexism, without sacrificing too much of their happiness, or betraying their dignity as women." Good advice . . . but it's hard to find much evidence of these important, incremental shifts in human evolution—the slow, slow path to peace—among the daily headlines that thundered a more oppressive reality.

The profound discomfort of alienation is both inevitable and necessary during periods of social change. It prods the desire to invent another kind of civilization: "When one comes to the end of a certain sense of illusions, one must find a new reason to go on, to reinvent the mechanism of dreaming," writer and artist Breyten Breytenbach said. "When the illusions are exhausted, one must replenish them. One *must*." But to be radically alienated is "extremely painful and can generate an anger so intense that it becomes immobilizing," Professor Morgan noted. Marginalized citizens are vulnerable to the paralysis of the blues, or worse, mobilized in the wrong direction: depressed women starve themselves into smaller sizes, frustrated men join militias and start shooting.

If the press actually did its whole job and supplied not only the facts but the context and meaning of the news, bystanders would be able to see their place in the scheme of things and take responsible action. If the Indiana media had put all the facts together, the big picture of "personal responsibility" would have looked like a slow form of infanticide, American-style: Denying welfare mothers medical coverage for abortions, then denying aid to future children, what would the governor have these mothers do? Breast-feed their babies while frying hamburgers at McDonald's?

The hard facts on the front page are directly related to the soft news from the home front, but it takes persistence to put them together: When you sell $23 billion in weapons every year, buyers will eventually use them—90 percent of the time on civilians; the good news on Wall Street about our profitable munitions industry is bad news in city emergency rooms, where the leading cause of death among male adolescents is gunshot wounds. If the media were to hold that picture—at least long enough for investors to think twice about where to put their money and Physicians for Social Responsibility to know where to aim their anger—it might accelerate the process of change.

The information bystanders receive from the media is further handicapped by an objectivity formula that quotes "experts" from both sides—a government official, a company spokesman—whose statements are rarely identified as lies. *Time* magazine published a startling 1994 photograph of seven CEOs in the tobacco industry, suited up and standing in a line with their right hands raised, taking an oath to tell the truth. Immediately afterward, they testified to Congress that "nicotine is not addictive." Two years later, Congress commissioned an investigation about whether the men had committed perjury. Could it be that, after two decades of wrangling with the Surgeon General's office, the leaders of the tobacco industry didn't *know*?

While the practice of objectivity was initiated to cure the "yellow journalism" that infected political reporting in the past, it has created other distortions today by pretending "both sides" are equally true. Homer Bigart, whose electrifying dispatches from Vietnam usually conflicted with Pentagon disinformation, loathed the policy at the *New York Times* that confused readers by printing both versions and letting the reader split the difference. Bigart called the practice "clerkish" and asked: "How can a fact and a lie both be correct? . . . Aren't we supposed to choose?" The media ducks this weighty responsibility when it publishes as much spin as substance, without distinction, essentially throwing their responsibility to readers: *you* figure it out.

At the beginning of each broadcast on Rush Limbaugh's television show, for example, he bows briefly to responsibility by announcing that some of what he says is serious and some of it is bullshit, and it's up to viewers to know the difference. But the camera never catches a member of the audience in a reflective frown, and the dittoheads laugh on cue. In a country so invested in the national game of "Let's Pretend" that we elected an actor to play president not once but twice, it shouldn't be a shock that a stand-up comic has become our leading political philosopher. A guy who just wants to have fun, Limbaugh distanced himself from any blame when some of his bewildered herd mistook comedy for marching orders. He meant all that bigotry and intolerance he broadcasts as pure entertainment.

Imagining a world beyond Us and Them, Carl Rogers described a "species politics" that replaced jargon with meaning, competition with cooperation. Communication would flow "upward as well as downward," Rogers explained. "People want to be heard and to feel that they are heard; they want to express their feelings and judgments about the issues." In our democratic media, the upward communication today occurs mainly through polls, where the silent majority appear without faces or names. We are lumped together by our vital statistics—gender, religion, political affiliation, marital status. Our opinions are limited to yes-and-no answers to words chosen for us: Do you have confidence in the president? Do you favor abortion? Should the United States send troops to Haiti? Without opportunity to frame the questions for ourselves, we are asked whether we are for or against, to choose either/or. There are no shades of gray in the polls. Those with strong opinions who attempt to explain themselves in the margins appears as "undecided," when in fact, we are the frustrated thinkers giving ANSWERS NOT FOUND.

People who take the news personally are at a distinct disadvantage in the sound-bite culture of television, since they actually care about the issues. Those shell-shocked women of the seventies—Susan Brownmiller on rape, Louise Armstrong on incest, I myself on the topic of motherhood—became incomprehensible in this short-take method of communication. Every televised interview felt like a lie of omission. The Yale historian Robin Winks once said that writing history is "like nailing jelly to the wall." On television, the jelly is liquified completely and the wall is made of cellophane.

Ted Koppel invited writer Tim Beneke on *Nightline* after the New Bedford gang rape, asking him to explain the behavior of men. Beneke's book *Men on Rape* is a provocative compendium of male attitudes on sexual violence, and I remember being relieved to see him among the guests. I hoped he'd tell me how to help my sons rise above the conquest mentality. When the camera focused on him during the first round of introductions, he was looking down at the cradle of his folded hands, as if he would have liked to crawl into it. When he heard his name, he lifted his head slowly, heavily, as if it were weighted by some unnamed responsibility. As he looked out of my TV screen, I noticed his eyes were open a shade wider than they needed to be. I thought I detected the edge of panic.

The last question of the evening was directed to Beneke. Bases loaded, he was in the cleanup position. After noting there were about twenty seconds left in the program, Ted asked: "Would any of this make any difference if the laws were changed?" Tim stared wildly into the camera, losing a few precious seconds. He knew too much, had done too much investigation into the minds and hearts of men. He lost a few more seconds. The he said. "We have to mobilize our wills so that at every step of the male socialization process men learn that it's not okay to rape." In twenty seconds, he could not give examples. He said we have to change the way we think, asking for no less than a cultural metanoia. I assumed nobody knew that he was talking about. You had to read the book.

I knew exactly what his panic felt like. I remember watching the women demonstrators on the steps outside the senate when Anita Hill finished her testimony. Reporters shoved microphones into the face of one startled woman, asking for a statement about what she thought about the hearings. Please, please, please make sense, I whispered as the shocked woman tried to phrase a twenty-second thought. But she sputtered incoherently, just as I would have, wearing the helpless frustration of a Woman Who Notices Too Much.

Writers, those poor ink-stained wretches driven to find the meaning of our human affairs, make terrible talk-show guests. The only thing viewers will find out about us on television is that we're easily flabbergasted. The worst crime you can commit on talk shows: boredom. It's no fun to watch someone deep in thought, so most guests are obliged to speak without it. In green rooms across America, guests are coached to interrupt and argue—display some "TV energy"—since that's the given formula for broadcast conversations. Talk shows are like Wrestling Mania, where opposing sides erupt with fake indignation and reel from artificial blows. Writers are wimps at this verbal sport.

"Do you know what your problem is on talk shows?" my friend Carrie asked during a critique after my appearance on the *Today* Show.

"Please . . . tell me," I said.

"You really try to answer the question. You try to *talk*." She reminded me that morning talk shows are not *My Dinner with Andre*. Nobody talks on TV the way we do around kitchen tables or over drinks, when we are getting down to the heart of what matters. What happens on TV is entertainment, where the news gets charmed. A spell is cast over our social issues: Everything must be fixed in three easy steps, so we can go on with the rest of the program. After the commercial break, viewers might be returned to another part of the set, where Martha Stewart is effortlessly filling a hundred pastry puffs. You can't get stuck thinking about the rapes in Bosnia—people have to leave for work.

My work as a cultural reporter has confirmed again and again that we Americans are much more complicated than what the stereotypes and narrow grids of "both sides" sug-

gest. It's been my job to track the slogans of our manufactured reality into the daily lives of actual people, where all
things are true but only partly true. My assignments over
the years have required me to penetrate the subcultures of
America far outside the Beltway, to explore how government, corporate, and economic policies look and feel in our
neighborhoods, churches, school rooms, subways; our
kitchens, our family rooms, our bedrooms. I have lived or
worked for months at a time with coal miners in Indiana
coming to terms with affirmative action, agoraphobic
mothers trying not to panic on Three Mile Island, New
York physicians staffing guerrilla clinics in the AIDS under-
ground, grassroots feminists raising consciousness in the
heartland, rural bankers funding microenterprise projects
in Alabama. It's been my job to learn their stories, understand their experience, translate local jargon into a common
language. Most of these special-interest groups are perceived to be outside the mainstream of "normal Americans," though they seemed perfectly normal, sometimes
even heroically normal, to me. Few people exactly fit the
stereotypes they're assigned—the guerrilla physicians were
impressively credentialed and certified, many blue collar
workers understood discrimination better than their white
collar supervisors—yet the belief in stereotypes outside our
own group persists. It will never be easy for our many dis-
parate subcultures to co-exist without friction, but neither is
it impossible. The first step toward Rogers's species politics
is to recognize that Us and Them are part of the same body
politic.

If business keeps profiting while labor keeps losing,
who will buy all those cars and pantyhose? If people with
pre-existing conditions stop existing altogether, who will
fill the waiting rooms for all those doctors? After decades of
squaring off as opposing sides, it takes imagination and
nerve to break through the Us/Them divide. But as Ber-

nice Johnson Reagon of Sweet Honey in the Rock, a female vocal group who sing a cappella, said, "If you're in a coalition and you're comfortable, you know it's not a broad enough coalition."

Because of our fragmented news, we Americans are all stationed at different parts of our elephantine politics, denying each other's reality. In truth, we aren't all in possession of the same facts, certainly not the same big picture. It's essential that we comprehend the meaning of our separate special interests, especially since one virtual reality eventually oozes into others. The members of the National Rifle Association are not just a vague annoyance when they send enrollment forms to the high school graduates of Fairfield County—including my very own sons.

Did Bernice Johnson Reagon mean our coalitions should be broad enough to include the Michigan militia? Even if to know them isn't to love them, if I understand the Norms of America would they be less terrifying? The University of Texas explored this question recently when representatives of special interest groups were selected for an innovative, three-day "pre-deliberation poll." Participants were relieved of their identifying labels and assigned to small groups that mixed together republicans and democrats, conservatives and liberals, prolife and pro-choice advocates, single and married people, men and women. Each group was given a list of social issues and a whole weekend to develop opinions, then report them in their own words.

The talks were discussions rather than debates because there were no sides—there were only people with a wide variety of experiences who had to tell their stories, explain their values, give their opinions. The experiment yielded some astonishing results. One conservative Christian woman from the South said the stories she heard from the other citizens in her group altered her understanding of abortion legislation. They did not change her pro-life position, but expanded it beyond a fetal view. "Why bring a life into the world only to suffer and die?" she asked after talking to the new friends she met in Austin, people she'd known mainly by rumor before.

What if the Austin experiment of pre-deliberation polling caught on? Suppose we all put down our guns for a week and came to the beach, viewed the horizon with the clarity of a three year old and started talking. Would we begin to understand that white or black, gay or straight, rich or poor, we all needed the same things . . . instead of Us or Them, would a species politics of Us *and* Them have a prayer?

VI

"A Beautiful Day in the Neighborhood"

AFTER LIVING IN so many subcultures of America, I could no longer identify "home" as a singular place. Home wasn't so much a place anymore as a psychological ground—for me, home was where my friends and family lived. I belonged not to a location but to a folk society, as anthropologist Robert Redfield described the human impulse to aggregate with one's own kind. Maybe in this flocking instinct, we are not so different from the cranes. My folk society was a nomadic tribe of longtime friends and activists, now spread from San Francisco to New York with heavy concentrations across the plains. Over the last twenty-five years, I've served as a foot soldier in the civil rights movement, the women's movement, the peace movement, and the green movement in Illinois, Indiana, Michigan and Connecticut. I have been, as John Kenneth Galbraith once told Jane O'Reilly, "an ardent supporter of all the great losing battles" of my times.

Though most of my former war buddies and I made valiant efforts to keep in touch by mail, fax, and phone, we all had nineties lives: too much to do, not enough time, and too many forms from tax accountants, insurance agents, podiatrists, school clerks, licensing bureaus, banks, colleges, and mileage programs to fill out—forget about coupons and junk mail. Everyone I know needs a personal Paperwork Reduction Act. So it was a thrill last summer to be back in the neighborhood of longtime friends, within driving distance for leisurely dinners and weekend overnights.

Since everyone in my folk society takes politics as personally as I do, we hadn't just raised our consciousness together over the last quarter century. We had also raised our kids together, held each other in emergency rooms, led cheers for each other's work. So when we hit the beaches together last summer, we had a lot of mutual territory to cover. We laughed, harumphed, consoled, empathized . . . each visit brought another little piece of forgotten history back into focus. During those first few months in Michigan, spending time with these friends was like coming home.

By the end of the summer, however, the creeping sense of alienation began rising again. I seemed to be only historically home—my present reality was going on without me in New York. Back in the heartland, everything was a few beats off from where it had been before. The place had changed a little, but I had changed a lot. I began missing New York, the manic capital of America. This was hard for some of my midwestern friends to understand.

Their perception of the place that I now called home came mainly from newspapers and movies. They pictured me in daily peril from drug addicts and murderers, not to mention deli countermen. In fact, the good people living in New York far outnumber the headline makers, despite their near extinction in the news. There is plenty of kindness in Manhattan—although the nurturance there, like everything else, is aggressive. Concerns are often barked as orders: "You're taking a cab," Carrie said, stuffing me into one outside the Time-Life building late one night after I'd told her I was walking home. "Don't make me worry about you." The bruising reputation of New Yorkers is largely untrue—everyone from the doormen to the colleagues who introduce you to "the people upstairs" know exactly how much help we all need, and regularly offer generous quantities of it. Affections feel brusque to new arrivals from Iowa or Georgia because everything moves faster—help is dispensed swiftly, without elaborate sentiment, because there's always someone right behind you needing something too.

Even though most of my midwestern friends have visited me in Manhattan—enjoyed Broadway plays and ethnic restaurants, had wonderful conversations with my friends, still laugh about the street exchanges in a city where everybody is a stand-up comic—this lived experience was less powerful than the images of violence and chaos coming through the framed views.

New Yorkers, of course, have the same skewed perception of the Midwest. Those who have traveled through instead of over these plain states on their way to Los Angeles may have stopped on the shores of the Great Lakes long enough to feel the peculiar expansion in their chest, been dazzled nearly to tears by the sheer beauty of sky and water, touched by the genuine friendliness and helpfulness of store clerks and waitresses. But while these experiences may have given them a hundred reasons why this region came to be called "the heartland," this lived reality is nevertheless dominated by images of a deer hunter run amok, stories about the Ku Klux Klan. Say "Midwest" in New York, they imagine Norm Olsen and the Michigan Militia.

Although I had already been working in New York for more than a decade by the time I finally moved there, I still felt I was entering yet another subculture I didn't wholly understand. I had grave apprehensions about finding enough members of my folk society to feel at home, especially after the newly elected leaders of both the city and state were speaking the same "personal responsibility" language that gave me the shivers from the Contract guys in Washington. Most of my New York colleagues were stricken with some strain of West Sider Depression that year, and I knew I was vulnerable too. I had made a few thousand commutes into the city by then, but I didn't really see it as a resident until I looked through the window of the moving van.

I remember clutching the handle next to the passenger's seat of the large U-Haul truck as it bounced through construction barricades on the Cross-Bronx Expressway, listening to my cargo crash against the walls as Howard, knuckles white with tension, swung the loose steering wheel to keep us on course. Sheer guts had put him in the driver's seat. This man, from whom I've now been divorced a little longer than the decade we were married, inspired groans from our teenage sons with his contentment at driving 55 mph on interstate highways. Ryan and Darren, the main glue between us for nearly twenty years, were following in the car behind, all of us exhausted and a little slap-happy after lifting and toting since dawn.

It was well past midnight on that steamy summer night in 1994, and I was acutely aware that this was "the first day of the rest of your life." Certainly, it was destined to be the last day of life as I'd known it. A recently paroled mother/writer/suburbanite, I was about to begin a solo life, the first time in forty-seven years I would not have to filter every decision through the needs and expectations of other people. The irony of having my once-husband and two former dependents launch me into independence made this surreal journey somehow more provocative.

The close relationships in our postnuclear family continually baffled friends, but I wasn't surprised when Howard called from Ann Arbor and volunteered his two-week vacation to help me pack my emptying nest in Connecticut. The sturdy friendship we retrieved from our divorce was rebuilt slowly from the powerful alloy of regret and apology, an interactive chemistry that eventually produces genuine change. We'd never imagined, when we naively recited those vows to love and honor each other for life back in 1970, we would mainly be providing each other unlimited opportunities for mercy.

Mercy is the antidote for the crushing pain that invariably follows the loss of innocence, and only the numb don't need it. Most recently, Howard had to forgive the hard time I gave him with *American Mom*, the memoir I'd just finished on twenty years of motherhood. Long familiar by now with the public compromises of an ex-wife-who-writes, he said reading the manuscript made him feel "like a jerk or a fool." When I asked him to identify the offending passages, it took him three weeks before he called back.

"It wasn't what you wrote that made me feel like a fool," he said quietly, utterly undefended. "It's my *life* I wish I could revise." Only in hindsight was it clear how he'd taken this fork instead of that, how decisions made in Michigan affected people he loved in Connecticut. Growing instead of shrinking from the truth, he understood we had no control, of course, over what other people would do with it.

The first review had arrived by fax that morning, shortly before I unplugged and packed the machine. I asked if the noxious label that would be appearing next to his name again and again had hurt. "Yeah," he admitted, "it got to me." He smiled ruefully, said he'd had a sudden image of us appearing together on a *Geraldo* show: "Deadbeat Dads and the Women Who Love Them." We laughed. Then we kept moving.

"How much room have I got on the right?" Howard yelled above the knocking engine. There is *no* room on the Right for guys like you, I thought, but dutifully checked the mirror and tried to sound confident: "At least a foot," I yelled back. These are perilous times for anyone living outside "the traditional family," since the reigning politicians are determined to bring us all back to the fifties. Certainly, the contemptuous labels we've had to live under—broken home, latchkey children, absentee mother, deadbeat dad—make it difficult for outsiders to recognize all the thinking and striving most postnuclear families do.

I knew that if the Contract with America proceeded as planned, my family and most of the people we care about were in for a siege. We're all named somewhere on the "enemies list": feminists, union organizers, poor people, agnostics, secular humanists, bleeding hearts, homosexuals, public-school children, the unemployed, the homeless, artists who aren't Norman Rockwell, sex educators, social workers, college students dependent on government loans, the mentally ill, welfare mothers, single mothers, divorced mothers, working mothers—actually, any mother who ventures outside of home—as well as the 39 million Americans without health insurance. Once all these "special-interest groups" are sifted out, the few citizens still standing when the family-values evangelists address "we Americans" are mainly white, rich, powerful Christians who are determined to inherit the earth and disinclined to share.

It's more than a little frightening to see how swiftly the Contract guys have revived the old formula for ridding a country of its conscience during hard economic times: First, you label whole segments of the population as the Other. Then, when the suffering comes, it's possible to believe they deserved it. If any of your own relatives turn out to be among the despised populations—a gay son, maybe, a divorced sister—well, mercy is notably absent from the current roster of family values.

Since the neighborhood I was moving into was teeming

with Others—accented immigrants, hyphenated-Americans, single moms, low-income families—I knew that casualties from the Contract on America would be falling within my direct line of vision. As Howard took the exit on the Upper West Side and aimed the truck down Broadway, I looked out the window at the street people I'd driven past hundreds of times, but never as a neighbor. What did being a "good neighbor" mean in this community, where the utterly destitute and fantastically wealthy live within blocks of each other?

How would I stay in touch with reality, when the daily reality is so unreal? Do I put on an arm band, own my affinity with the Others—or do I wear mental blinders, try not to know what I know? Pummeled by questions, I felt a tremendous shudder slice through me. I suppose I knew then I was doomed to be part of the resistance. In the open psychiatric wards of Manhattan sidewalks, I was a readily identifiable "Sucker Man," as Darren would say in sticky situations, remembering a childhood toy with suction cups that glowed in the dark.

I used to make panhandler rules whenever I came into the city—I would give to the sick but not the addicted, the humble but not the rude, the old but not the young. Eventually, I just gave to anyone who asked. It was much easier than trying to figure out how rude or crazy I might become if I lived on the streets. Jonathan Raban was briefly transported into the panhandler's reality when he took a break from his interviews one day and sat down on a fire hydrant. Given "an exaggeratedly wide berth" by pedestrians, he tried to make eye contact, managing "to catch a few pairs of pupils offguard; they swerved away in their sockets, as quick as fish. It was interesting to feel oneself being willed into nonexistence by total strangers. I'd never felt the force of such frank contempt—and all because I was sitting on a fire hydrant. Every one of these guys wanted to see me wiped out. I was a virus, a bad smell, a dirty smear that needed cleaning up. After only a minute or two of this, I began to warm with reciprocal feeling; had I stayed on my hydrant for an hour, I'd have been aching to get my fist round a tire iron or the butt of a .38, just to let a zombie know that I was human too."

Howard had acquired a new nickname that week after he dropped a 27-inch TV a customer had brought in for repairs. "Hey, Crash!" the wise guys he worked with would greet him, "How's it goin'?" With all my material possessions in the U-Haul, I had nothing to lose with Crash at the wheel, since my alternate driver was Anthony, the Connecticut neighbor who'd shorn the roof off a delivery van when he plowed into a sign that said, "Clearance—8'." ("Sure I saw it," he later told the hospital staff. "I forgot I was in the stupid truck.") I already missed Anthony, and the rest of the gang who regularly camped out around our kitchen table.

I loved that raucous household, blooming with growth and optimism. The quiet solitude after Ryan and Darren left for college felt abrupt. In truth, our quality time together was sometimes down to five minutes a day by then, and the main noise was running water. My landlady had been shocked by our water bills and asked if she should send a plumber to check for leaks.

"No," I confessed, "I'm growing male adolescents here. They need a lot of showers." I offered to pay the difference, since watering teenagers was more economical and effective than therapy, and ultimately easier on the environment. The boys would emerge in elevated moods, skin flushed and wrapped in terry cloth. Every time I would come across those alarming headlines about young male violence and try to imagine what might save us, I'd think: showers. If every kid in America had enough private time in the bathroom to get a grip, to feel just *great* for a moment . . . wouldn't it have to improve civilization?

I was lucky to find a "prewar" apartment, Manhattan shorthand for big rooms that haven't been subdivided into six studios with pantry kitchens and broom-closet bathrooms. Space is so precious in New York, custody suits over rent-controlled apartments are common when couples split up. After postwar prosperity devolved into today's social Darwinism, whole working-class families now read, watch TV, eat, make love, fight, cry, laugh, yell, and sleep all in the same room.

Driving through Harlem a few years earlier, I'd gotten lost in an urban canyon between tall, crumbling buildings. The narrow street was solidly double-parked, and I noticed every car was occupied: one man was reading by flashlight, another was having a cigarette, a pair of teenagers were car-dancing to a radio, another pair was sinking slowly to the seat. Here, on the streets, people were in the only private room at home. It's no wonder tempers flare and violence erupts during steamy summers in the city. Who can take a shower in a car?

My neighborhood is "in transition," as we say, between an elegant past and present cruelties, a microcosm of the growing class divisions in America. One block west of my building, uniformed doormen with epaulets safeguard well-to-do residents who are likely to be liberal, generous contributors to the soup kitchen in the nearby cathedral. One block east, crack vials litter the sidewalks where street people and drug addicts spend the night. The haves and have-nots live cheek by jowl here—with remarkable civility, I think, given the givens.

"Always, I noticed, I was addressed as 'sir,'" Raban noted. "In the great Depression, it had been 'Buddy, can you spare a dime?'; fifty years on, we were buddies no longer. *They* were the outcast; *I* was the tenant of an apartment . . . and there was no calling on my sense of fraternity to answer their need. I was sorry about the passage of that *buddy;* its disappearance registered something newly cruel in New York life." That this cruelty breeds crime could hardly be a surprise. What astonished me was the decency with which most petty crimes occurred. The thief who would eventually steal my car radio did not break any windows, and left a screwdriver behind on the seat. When the car was broken into again a week later, nothing was taken. Somebody evidently just needed a room.

My suburban habit of getting close to neighbors was trickier here because they come and go—sometimes within the same day. It was hard to learn all their names without mailboxes. And the names sometimes changed. The woman with the wild gray hair and bedroom slippers who growls at pedestrians on the west side of Broadway calls herself "Bad Bertha," but when she's sitting quietly on the east side, her hair tucked neatly into a bun and feet prettily aligned in ballet shoes, her name is "Irena." The exuberantly manic guy who works the street outside the Hungarian Pastry Shop calls himself "the Lord's apostle," and sings a gospel rap to marks that sounds like a kind of Gregorian "Dixie." One rhyme made me laugh—and a laugh in Manhattan is worth a buck to me: "I love Christ, Jesus Christ, The only Man who's been here twice . . ."

But there was a dramatic shift in my street relationships when Howard, the boys, and I were finishing renovations on the apartment. That whole week, nobody hit on us for money. Instead, panhandlers grinned and nodded when we passed them during errands and lunch breaks, as though we were old comrades. Maybe they only solicit suburban commuters, I thought, and now recognized us as neighbors. Then I realized it was because of how we were dressed: paint-splattered T-shirts, sweaty kerchiefs, shoes covered with sawdust and spackle. Crash's work outfit was truly special—Howard had grabbed a pair of old sweats from the Goodwill pile in Connecticut and didn't discover the cord was missing until he put them on in New York. We searched the vacant apartment for a piece of string or elastic, but all we came up with from work supplies was a roll of duct tape. Even the craziest panhandlers weren't tempted to solicit change from a guy wearing a cummerbund of silver duct tape.

If our degrees of separation could melt with a change of attire, perhaps the current experiment with Casual Days, when corporations relax formal dress codes on Fridays, should go even further. Maybe Mondays should be Down-in-the-Socks Day. Princely executives could become paupers once a week and get to know the folks who are so invisible to *Wall Street Journal* readers. In their starched collars and knotted ties and pressed twill, so many of the Suits who bustle down Broadway dodging strollers and shopping carts look either uncomfortable or angry, as if everybody wants their stuff. Most everybody probably does.

But suppose they relieved themselves of this burden once a week, surrendered their gabardine armor and leather belts for a Goodwill outfit and roll of duct tape. Would they be less angry if nobody was hitting on them? If they got grins and nods on the streets, if they made eye contact and learned the names of the Others, would they be tempted to open up membership in the tight little group of "we Americans?" It's almost too poignant to imagine, but could the in-it-together camaraderie on the streets even move the Contract guys to share their drugs? The comprehensive health coverage for Congress and the military is costing taxpayers a bundle, but that entitlement program never appears on the Republican's list of "financial burdens."

Party strategist William Kristol had chastised GOP colleagues for compromising their economic goals after Democrats launched an offensive campaign with the "poli-

tics of compassion" during the last presidential election.
Addressing a *National Review* conference on C-SPAN after
losing the election, he warned his fellow Republicans not to
be sidetracked by worries about poor people next time. If
the rich could become richer still, objections to ruthlessness
would become moot: "The politics of growth trump the
politics of compassion," he declared over and over. Greed
trumps mercy every time. It was late at night when I heard
this game plan in my hotel room almost four years ago. I
couldn't think of anyone to call, anything to do. Now Kristol is the chairman of Project for the Republican Future and
his colleagues have taken Capitol Hill. Should I have called
911?

My tired moving crew, after unloading and returning the
truck, crashed on mattresses flush with the floors and didn't
get up until noon the next day. Then, muscles sore but
freshly showered, we were in elevated moods after lunch
in a local Chinese-Cuban restaurant. "Chinese-Cuban-
Americans," I said, wondering how I would ever keep track
of the hyphens in New York. "Imagine fleeing the Gang of
Four and landing in Castro country."

"Yeah," Howard said, "then risking your life in an open
boat and washing up here just in time for the Gingrich
Gang." Ryan and Darren gave each other a worried look,
familiar by now with their progenitors' habit of getting
worked up over politics. They hated hearing about suffering they couldn't do anything about. If we were going to
saddle them with family values of mercy and justice in these
mean times, they wanted to know how to fend off despair.
Though we were not regular churchgoers—the religion in
our postnuclear family is an interfaith amalgam of Catholic
beatitudes and Lutheran heresies and Zen koans—I suggested a visit to St. John the Divine.

The largest Episcopal cathedral in North America, its

towering spire of magnificent masonry now sits sullenly under rusted iron scaffolding, renovations stalled once more while fund-raising efforts are applied to more immediate emergencies. Dean James Morton has the formidable task of convincing wealthy parishioners deeply committed to art and historic preservation that their first obligation, as Episcopalians, is to serve the community—in their case, ceaseless waves of troubled kids, addicted veterans, dying homosexuals, and homeless immigrants. In the turf wars between the Suits and the Others in this West Side Story, the cathedral is the parking lot where miracles happen.

Still beautiful despite its present humility, the stately edifice buzzes with civilian activity. Before New York adopted a recycling program, parishioners brought their garbage to church, where the homeless turned aluminum cans into cash. A masonry program now provides training and jobs for the unemployed as renovation teams from the cathedral, like barn-raising neighbors of the past, restore nearby tenements for the poor. The doors are open to anyone who wants in—on the Feast of St. Francis, when members bring pets to the procession honoring all God's creatures, even elephants come to St. John the Divine.

In the park next to the interfaith elementary school, we stopped before an installation by sculptor Frederick Franck. A row of six steel panels are aligned on the lawn perpendicular to the path, each with a silhouette of the same human figure cut from the center, the first one slightly larger than life, the last a miniature version of the shrinking figure itself. The inscription quotes the Great Law of the Haudenosaunee, the Six Nations Iroquois Confederacy: "In all our deliberations we must be mindful of the impact our decisions have on the seven generations to follow us." Franck titled the sculpture *Seven Generations*, but there are only six figures. The viewer, standing squarely at the mouth of the tunnel, must become the seventh. We each took turns

looking through the five ghostly silhouettes, connecting
with the tiny figure at the end. Step aside from your place in
the human chain, and it disappears.

I wondered how the Iroquois chiefs came to their
remarkably long view of personal responsibility. How did
they make the connection between their business decisions
in Michigan and domestic life in Connecticut? Were they
all in relationships with difficult squaws? Did they speak the
hard truth, argue and apologize, let mercy change them?
Seemingly larger than life in their war paint and head-
dresses, did the chiefs declare a Casual Day at the Haudenosaunee Council, light the pipe, and pass it around? Did
they inhale?

The architects of the Project for the Republican Future
can't be worried about the next seven generations—William
Kristol said it's not even practical to care about most of *this*
one. "You cannot in practice have a federal guarantee that
people won't starve," he told *Harper's* during a candid forum
with five other Contract guys, explaining how their plan
will work. Some people will have to suffer, but "that's just
political reality" said author David Frum. Apparently
unaware of Dean Morton's work with New York Episcopalians, Frum doesn't think "the sort of people who make
$100,000 contributions to the Republican party" can get
behind poor people. "Republicans are much more afraid of
angry symphony-goers than of people starving to death," he
said.

I can't agree, of course, that people with a talent for banking
have no gift for compassion. A few years after teaching me
the siren prayer, my father came along on a family shopping
trip to Chernin's, a discount shoe store then located on the
downtown fringe near Maxwell Street. He generally
depended on my mother to get all five of us outfitted for
Easter without his assistance, but he wasn't crazy about her

driving into this neighborhood without him. It was a novelty to have him along, and I stayed with him while he parked the car after he dropped our troops at the door. As we were crossing Maxwell Street, we stopped to watch the police load some drunks into a paddy wagon. It was a quiet scene, no protests or sirens, just a few lights flashing in broad daylight. But my father made the sign of the cross anyway, and his lips began moving silently.

"Why are you praying for *them?*" I asked. They weren't struggling for oxygen or watching their houses burn down. They didn't even have houses, and seemed unlikely candidates for grace.

"You pray for folks in *any* kind of trouble, Sis," my father said firmly, almost sharply. "Especially those poor fellows . . . ask God to bless them, and their families too." I'd never thought of these scary men as having families—I hardly thought of them as human. My father—a tall, trim bank officer, very nearly always suited except when he mowed the lawn or clipped the hedges—was as far removed from the human matter inside the paddy wagon as anyone could be. I didn't understand why he cared so much.

My father never talked much about his childhood during the decades he and my mother were raising their kids. I knew he was an "orphan" after the Great Depression, that his mother died shortly after his youngest brother was born, and he was raised by Gramma O'Leary, who was actually his aunt. I would only learn much later that his father had been alive, that his aunt would send him and his two young brothers to Skid Row whenever her home laundering business didn't bring in quite enough money. And my father would only learn much later, when medical science discovered a genetic connection for the mental illness that eventually claimed his eldest son, that maybe his alcoholic father had been suffering another, deeper disorder. I was too young and self-absorbed to understand I would eventually see my own beloved relatives in the mad, vacant faces of the street people. The only thing I knew for sure on Maxwell Street that day was that my father, still holding my hand, was no longer with me.

He stood staring into space for a few moments after his lips stopped moving. The human matter inside the paddy wagon seemed to reach out and take him. He was inside, riding away from me. Then he made the sign of the cross again and came to.

"C'mon, Sis," he said, finally launching us from the curb. "Let's go find your mother before I own all the shoes in the store." In truth, we both knew my mother was the disciplined, thrifty partner of their team during family excursions. My father was the soft touch when his guard was down, and I knew that afternoon those patent leather pumps without the straps were mine.

The main problem with running a merciless government is that in a democracy, millions of voters have to agree to starvation. This requires a certain "finesse," as media adviser Frank Luntz said. "I'll explain it in one sentence: I don't want to deliver bad news from a golf course in Kennebunkport." Republicans are depending on Rush Limbaugh, the undisputed master of political spin, to keep people dizzy and laughing about starvation plans. Labeling people like me "compassion fascists" for trying to get people like him interested in mercy, Limbaugh is so popular even the *New York Times* compromised its editors when marketing executives hired him to advertise the newspaper. In the new morality of bottom-liners, it's okay to have a propagandist represent the "newspaper of record" if it increases sales. Vice must be spun into virtue before the bystanders could consent to the newest power dream of our politicians, but everybody's doing their part.

Several years ago, Ivan Boesky spoke to students at the

University of California while on tour to promote his book. "Greed is healthy," he inspired them. "You can be greedy and still feel good about yourself." Boesky's invocation of avarice didn't stir any action from Republican crusaders fighting "moral depravity in public schools," which Pat Buchanan blamed on single moms and broken homes. Talk about a dazzling public relations coup: The party championing morality in America has declared that charity is impractical, green is healthy, compassion is fascist, and mercy is the responsibility of Other people. If future schoolchildren have to recite a prayer written by these folks, whatever will it say? "Dear God, please give me more of everything than I'll ever need, and I promise not to care about anyone else."

Though I'm not an Episcopalian, visiting St. John's always made me wish I could pray. I envy the solace my family and friends have in talking to God. My own spiritual meditations are generally addressed to Frank, the euphoric madman who left abruptly at age thirty-six, delirious with love and forgiveness as he answered God's call. I still want him to tell me: *Is* heaven better than the SRO where the Chicago police found his body? Sitting in the garden at St. John's, I remembered our last conversation on the lawn at Elgin State Hospital. He asked me why I loved him and I said, "Because you are a fool, and I love fools."

"But Jesus said, 'There are no fools,'" he replied, quoting a scriptural fragment from his seminarian days.

"I know," I replied. "But I think what Jesus really meant is that we are all fools," I said, quoting J. D. Salinger. I told him I thought he was the King of Fools. He laughed, said I must be the Queen.

I don't blame God for the scrambled thinking that led to Frank's suicide. I can't even be sure there is a God. I believe my divinely crazy brother heard God say what he wanted to hear. Many mentally ill people think they are in direct touch with the Almighty. The Lord's apostle outside the pastry shop, the toothless guy at D'Agostino's, even Bertha on her bad days will offer the panhandler's benediction: "God bless you," they say, whether the quarter comes or not.

Republican Christians today are getting some frenzied directives as the political scene becomes ever crazier, and they too hear exactly what they want to hear: God wants everybody to get married, wants women to stay home, doesn't want America in the U.N., doesn't want a capital gains tax. I can't share their faith that a supreme benevolence is behind all these messages, but if the polls are correct and most Americans think somebody's God should be directing all our lives, let's please not pick the one who's inspiring pro-lifers to get automatic weapons. Until we have a firmer grip on our common reality, maybe we could all follow the harmless god who's telling the autistic disciple on Thirty-fourth Street, over and over: "Go to Macy's nine-to-five, go to Macy's nine-to-five." We could leave the credit cards home, stay out of trouble. Just look.

The night before Howard and the boys returned to their respective lives in the Midwest, we treated ourselves to a leisurely dinner and then walked home. It was a beautiful summer night on Broadway and we were in high spirits, grateful there were no more boxes to move. When a U-Haul truck rattled down the street, Crash laughed and asked, "Do you think they'd have less business if the company was named 'U-Bust-Your-Ass'?" Our laughing foursome attracted looks from our neighbors, but few grinned or nodded, as if we'd become strangers again. Darren noticed too.

"This is too weird," he said. "People are staring at us because we look so *normal*. Like Mom and Pop and the two boys from Iowa." He was struck by the irony of having been labeled the weirdos in almost every neighborhood we've lived in, then arriving here—where weirdos abound—and being mistaken for regular guys.

"We should wear a sign," he said. "We're Not What You Think."

I thought everyone should wear that sign through the next election, since there's still so much confusion about the Other. As bad decisions in Washington crush good people in Harlem, even "liberal" politicians are telling us to prepare for further compromises—live a little leaner, do more charity work, tighten our belts. What can they be thinking? My neighbors are already living in cars, doing-it-yourself, holding pants up with duct tape. There is plenty of self-help and personal responsibility out here, where people watch each other's kids and take mostly working vacations, if we take them at all.

How did the Contract guys ever get the impression they are doing all the work? Because they are earning all the big bucks? Why are the Republicans so mad—why so furious with mothers? Do they need more Elavil? More Prozac? Since all the female labor sustaining them at home and at work is so invisible, so seemingly profitless, they can't seem to hold the picture that somebody's valuable work is responsible for the fact their children are alive, their Contracts are typed. The arrogance and ignorance of the current political leadership is so stupefying, you don't even want to argue with these boys—"you just want to *slap* them," as Molly Ivins wrote. Maybe that's why the welfare reformers loathe mothers so much—we remind them they have to share, take turns, *grow up*.

The next morning we loaded the roof of Howard's car so high with the boy's suitcases, sports equipment, easels, and trunks, we had to make one last trip to the hardware store for longer bungee cords. It was a hectic departure as the Clampetts hit the road, and I waved from the curb as they mouthed their final good-byes through the window. Still smiling, I stayed on the curb for a long time, sorry the party was over. Letting go rarely comes naturally to me, and I felt my worry reflexes kick in as the car turned the corner.

Almost every family value Howard and I have tried to give our sons will cause them nothing but trouble, if they choose to live them. As two young, educated white guys who could qualify as insiders if they got behind the Contract on the rest of us, there are bound to be days they'll feel like Sucker Man, stuck with mercy when greed was called trump. I know it's a peculiar wish for a mother, but I hoped they would never quite fit in with their crowd. Certainly their affinity with their dad, a truly original odd man out, was a heartening sign. I imagined them all laughing for the next 750 miles.

For months afterward, every time I walked past the cathedral I would remember that densely emotional departure, feel the same swell of love I'd had standing on the curb that morning. I'd look up at the scaffolded spire and wish I could pray. I would remember my religious instructor's belief that we were all fools, walking from one hallowed ground to the next. Dear God, I'd think, please . . . let us be merciful fools.

. . . WITH LIBERTY AND
JUSTICE FOR ALL.

◆

PART FOUR

The Revolt of the Bystander

VII

Bad Faith and True Believers

SINCE OUR DOMESTIC chaos has by now been documented in headlines from Canada to Japan, it's impossible for national leaders to suppose we Americans haven't noticed something's very wrong here, too. In the absence of military responsibility, corporate responsibility, media responsibility, government responsibility, and civic responsibility, the current campaign for "personal responsibility" is really political shorthand for "nobody's going to take any responsibility." With so much suffering, as American jobs are exported and violence keeps coming home, *somebody* has to take the heat. Enraged bystanders could become a revolutionary force if their anger is not capped or diverted.

The poor are handy scapegoats for problems in our crumbling cities, but they don't make it out to the suburbs often and the ones who do, as domestics or handymen, tend to be more welcomed than despised. The poor can hardly relieve the oceanic frustrations of the middle-class by exerting more "personal responsibility." And as the facts in the box start leaking out, more and more bystanders are realizing that the amount we spend on a single Pentagon disinformation program or corporate bailout could easily replace what we spend annually on welfare. Even if every welfare mother started frying hamburgers at a McDonald's tomorrow, the rest of us would still be working sixty-hour weeks in downsized corporations, still be worrying about what our kids are watching on television.

Under the mounting stress of disappearing wages and oppressive to-do lists, the quality of American family life has deteriorated so badly we need a scapegoat that can bear the whole weight of our domestic unhappiness . . . and we all know who's responsible for that. Honoring a long-standing American tradition, right-wing leaders of the "pro-family" movement have declared "Let's blame it on Mom."

In the virtual reality of the family-values evangelists, the superior virtue of the nuclear family—with its traditional homemaker and breadwinning father—is being undermined by a growing number of deviants. Many studies from the Heritage Foundation and the Christian Coalition have amassed statistics to prove that the economy is not working, our morality has been shredded, because of Them. The enemies include not only the usual suspects—gays and lesbians, career women, feminists—but worse, a whole lot of formerly normal Americans who have drifted from tradition as well. To restore both morality and the good life in America, everyone must get back into a nuclear family. Anyone who splits from this atomic structure can now be held in contempt and charged with a kind of domestic treason.

In what Pat Buchanan described as a cultural war for the soul of America, Christian fundamentalists are pushing a political agenda that will make life more difficult for single moms, divorced moms, working moms, welfare moms and lesbian moms (double points for quotable attacks on the latter two). According to leaders of the pro-family movement, normal Americans do not have sex, do not have children, outside the institution of marriage. With these criteria for admission to God's country—unless everyone lies on the application forms—America will be shrinking to the size of Conway, Michigan.

In the national game of "Let's Pretend," the issues we're not supposed to talk about and the truths we have to pretend we don't know are ever more incredible: former Surgeon General Joycelyn Elders was pressured to resign after mentioning "masturbation" during a public discussion of safe-sex practices. Apparently, we're now pretending the good people of America don't masturbate. The president of the United States actually announced, under pressure from the family-values faction for his official position on masturbation, that "he didn't approve of the practice." Our president thinks he has to pretend to believe this stuff for us Americans, knowing he'll be speaking in *France* next month. Really . . . we seem intent on proving to the world that every stereotype of American hypocrisy and buffoonery is true. Elders got the ax because she had the unfortunate job of speaking frankly about sex in America, where it is widely believed that if you don't talk about it, it isn't happening. Keep the herd bewildered . . . because information is power.

It's hard to believe that in 1996 bystanders could support a politics that spreads contempt for abnormal Americans living outside the nuclear family—since the vast majority of us do—but here we go again, as our favorite president used to say. A thick file from my Blue Box contains the many grievances against "nontraditional" families: Christian Coalition president Ralph Reed, undisturbed that all the female-headed households sliding into poverty might be the result rather than cause of our dismal economy, told a *Harper's* forum that single mothers owed it to taxpayers—if not to God—to get married and stay married. Author George Gilder, the author of *Sexual Suicide* and a leading philosopher of the pro-family movement, blames unmarried career women for male violence and offers anthropological evidence that men, untethered from a civilizing female influence and the yoke of family obligations, have practically no choice but to rape, pillage, and generally destroy society. And in a cover story in the *Atlantic*, Barbara DaFoe Whitehead amassed impressive statistics to prove that children living with two parents are better off than children living with one—they inherit more money, live in nicer homes, have superior medical care, get better educations, marry earlier. She then offers many unpleasant suggestions about how to reform "selfish Americans" who "changed their minds about staying together for the sake of the children." Since it's mainly women who choose divorce over death-do-us-part, we know which feckless Americans she means. On the apparent belief that we could all live like June and Ward and Wally and the Beaver if women just stayed married, Whitehead proposes the way to national salvation is to "restigmatize divorce."

As a longtime veteran of the struggling legion of divorced, working moms in this country, I was naturally depressed that the breakdown of American civilization is being pinned on me. I supposed I could feel flattered that my little army of irregulars is considered threatening enough to bring the most powerful country in the world to its knees. But few working moms can indulge that conceit because, in truth, it's our knees that are in constant danger of buckling, since we're bearing more weight and working longer hours than almost any other segment of the population.

God knows, the institution of the family needs drastic reform—ever since the Cold War began fifty years ago, politicians have depended on "the American family" to quietly absorb the spills of military violence and the psychological despair of prolonged unemployment. The lies and secrecy that permeated business and government during those years also infiltrated private lives. The protective screen of "private family matters," like the defense shield of "national security," has obscured all kinds of foul deeds. Before General Colin Powell withdrew his name from the list of presidential contenders, he said he would return us to civility by running the country "like a family." Like which American family, I wondered. Susan Smith's?

In her trial for criminal neglect after the drowning of her two young sons, her defense attorneys argued that Smith's own upbringing hadn't provided much example for how to raise a family: her father committed suicide when she was six years old; her mother refused psychological counseling for her when she herself attempted suicide as a teenager; and her stepfather, Beverly Russell, "a loud-praying leader of both the Christian Coalition and the GOP in South Carolina," had, according to the *Washington Spectator*, molested her since she was fifteen and engaged her in what the press called "consensual sexual relations" in the months before the drowning.

Her own husband, David Smith, who began an affair when she was pregnant with their child, later admitted in his memoir that it was probably "hurtful" to "step out" on a woman when she was so "vulnerable." And Smith's well-to-do lover, Tom Findlay, had dumped her because he didn't want any responsibility for her dependent children. None of these extenuating circumstances—desertion, incest, infidelity, and abandonment—ultimately absolved her of guilt. The grim facts in my Blue Box reveal that most Americans have experienced at least one of these traumas somewhere in their history. Susan Smith was not different because of her private family matters, only more extreme. The day she drove to the edge of the lake she was an impoverished, exhausted, suicidal product of a not-so-atypical American family.

While the country had divided sympathies for the athlete charged with murdering his wife, there was no ambiguity in the public outrage for the mother who drowned her children. The two simultaneous trials revealed deep prejudices and fears in the body politic: Men who battered wives might be criminals, but crowds of supporters did not find their behavior incomprehensible and had "reasonable doubts." Women who drowned their children were so far outside the criminal norm, the public was uniformly stupefied and demanded the death penalty.

"I would have taken those boys in a heartbeat," one neighbor had said, if only Susan Smith had asked for help. Except mothers are not supposed to need help. As David Smith wrote in his subsequent memoir, "one thing I can fault Susan for—and as I've said, in all other respects she was a good mom to Alex and Michael—was that she had this tendency to leave the boys at other people's houses while she went about her business." David Smith, the man who couldn't even get through his wife's pregnancy without stepping out, thought this proved his wife was lacking the normal maternal instinct. Had there been some recognition that a woman with a history of depression and suicide might need guilt-free, drop-off child care for a few hours, maybe this final tragedy in a long chain of nuclear family reactions might have been prevented.

Even with all the shocking evidence of what's been going on behind closed doors, myths about the superiority of "the traditional family" continue to be stronger than our grip on reality. "It is funny and a bit pathetic that Ronald and Nancy Reagan keep finding out their family secrets by reading their children's books," Delia Ephron remarked in a *New York Times* review of Maureen Reagan's memoir. "It is also ironic that this couple who symbolized a return to hearth, home and 1950s innocence should, in reality, be candidates for a very 1980s study on the troubled family." Sociologist

Judith Stacey found it astonishing that our actor president, "despite his own divorce and his own far-from-happily blended family (with) his *second* lady, managed to serve so effectively as symbolic figurehead of a pro-family agenda which his economic and social policies helped further undermine."

Some of the most impassioned speeches about family values today are coming from House Speaker Newt Gingrich and radio host Rush Limbaugh, both of whom seem to have forgotten that they, too, are divorced. It's apparently not husbands leaving their wives that has the Christian Coalition in such a froth—it's wives striking out for independence that's so threatening to national security.

Since the favored solution to every social problem today is to build more penitentiaries, it's probably only a matter of time before someone suggests jailing single mothers. Actually, family court judge Wayne Creech of Columbia, South Carolina, stopped just short of that in a decision he handed down last December to Tonya Harter, a fifteen-year-old girl with a history of juvenile delinquency. Creech ordered her to be "chained to her mother—twenty-four hours a day, seven days a week—for a month," the *New York Times* reported. "Under his ruling, if the girl is caught unshackled, her mother faces 30 days in prison."

"This is a very stressful situation that judge has put me in," said Deborah Harter, Tonya's thirty-eight-year-old mother. Chained together, she and her daughter "go everywhere together—to school, to the store, to bed, to the bathroom." This wasn't the first time Judge Creech, frustrated by the intractable problem of juvenile delinquency, chained a mother to her children. After his research turned up no state or federal law prohibiting this unusual punishment, he decided that parents must take responsibility or face a prison sentence . . . though the hasn't yet chained any children to their fathers.

* * *

The nuclear family is imploding under today's social stresses and yet, instead of expanding options and releasing the pressure, we are on the same MAD path we chose before, clinging to a compulsory family structure that brings the police state home. Deborah Harter was described by the *Times* as "a homemaker," so even traditional mothers are not exempt during the campaign to put women back in chains again. Imagine what her one-month sentence might have been if she were one of the deviant moms.

It will be difficult for most married women to see the connection between Us and Them in the heated rhetoric of the cultural war, but the program to restigmatize divorce will have a profoundly negative effect on those who remain married. Marriage and divorce are parallel institutions, and the living conditions in one have a direct impact on those in the other. It may not be immediately obvious to righteous traditionalists, but the survival of ex-wives is critical to the happiness of still-wives. By restricting divorce, the message that goes out to negligent husbands and abusive fathers is this: Be mean, be brutal, do whatever you want—your wife can't leave. In a culture where independent mothers were visibly thriving, however, the message would be this: Better talk, better listen, better not take her for granted—she can live quite satisfactorily without you.

The stigmatization plan hardly seems necessary— maybe I missed some amnesty period, but my sons and I have lived under denigrating labels for most of their lives. Trust me: the experts can relax about divorced moms feeling too good about ourselves. Still, as punishing as life can be out here on the frontiers of the nuclear family, few of us would go back. The alternative to divorce is not a happy, or even a merely solvent, marriage—for some women, the alternative was a fatal one.

Author Joan Frank remembers the mother who was among the casualties of the fifties, the last time the Plan was in effect: "In that day there was great, shameful stigma attached to any hint of even having sought counseling—much better to hide the black eye, the crushed heart. Here is how a family friend describes the lot of women then: 'You just injected your grapefruit with vodka and shut up.'" For a woman trapped in a loveless marriage, without access to money controlled by her husband, unable to support two young daughters on the pitiful wages listed under "female jobs" in the want ads, there was "no way out . . . at least not to one so purely and comprehensively exhausted," Frank wrote. "As if hanging from a high ledge by fingertips, her grip finally, simply, gave." The bottle of pills next to her mother's limp body were never discussed after the funeral. You didn't talk about "private family matters" in the fifties.

In our domestic police state, marriages-as-prison won't provide maximum security—there were still quite a few escapees even in the rigid fifties. But psychological prisons have the advantage of being cheaply constructed through social pressure. "Stigmatization is a powerful means of regulating behavior, as any smoker or overeater will testify," Whitehead observed—as if the need for divorce were in the same category with cravings for a hot fudge sundae. Few of us who have actually been through the ordeal see ourselves as addicted—quite the contrary in fact.

A few years ago I visited a friend shortly after her divorce, and watched the real life of the "wanton divorcee." Coming from a demanding new job where tenure was still a question and a much-needed raise depended on a yes, Alice continued moving nonstop all evening—making a pot roast, washing dishes, doing laundry, solving her younger daughter's problems at the computer, helping her older daughter with a college loan application, making arrangements for car repairs, being patient, patient, patient. Taking pains to be "emotionally available" to her daughters, she worried that she'd been too preoccupied with her dissertation last year and her divorce this year. I watched her tight control all evening, seeing myself after my own life had gone completely to hell. Doing the work of two people for the income of half a person, single mothers needed every crumb of affirmation a day could yield.

I once thought there could be no more awful pain than knowing you must leave someone you've loved—but the aftermath of shattered love in an unforgiving culture was punishing beyond belief. When Professor Whitehead looked at our lives through her statistics, she came up with "selfish." If she could have come into Alice's kitchen and heard the actual story, the grief and the love and the deep, dark wit, she might have come to another conclusion.

But whether divorced women are selfish or courageous is ultimately beside the point, because we are necessary. The quality of family life cannot be improved—especially if the luxury of love is to be involved in future marriages—without the option of divorce. While the family-values folks interpret the rising divorce rate as a dismal sign that self-absorbed women are not doing their duty, I read it from the opposite shore and see a hopeful sign that we are raising the bar, refusing to surrender our lives to unhappy, abusive, or demeaning marriages.

It took several thousand years before marriage evolved from a sexual and economic arrangement that guaranteed paternity and inheritances to a human partnership that included love. This modern addition changed the practice of marriage immeasurably, because love—impervious to demands or contracts—can only be earned, day after day. In *Brave New Families*, Judith Stacey's study of working-class families in Silicon Valley, one subject said she left a first marriage that provided a home, a car, and the steadily rising income of a professional husband because it no longer met her new criteria. What had been missing? the sociologist asked.

"It's real easy," she replied. "Self-respect."

In a national survey on marital satisfaction commissioned by *Woman's Day* several years ago, two of the most frequent complaints from unhappy wives were "He takes me for granted" and "He doesn't talk." Half of these depressed women were not planning to divorce, since they didn't regard these complaints as "legitimate" reasons. If self-respect and good communication were to become grounds for divorce, of course, those qualities would start appearing more frequently in ongoing marriages as well. A 50 percent divorce rate means that everybody, inside and outside of wedlock, has to start talking.

"You get the same kind of divorce as the marriage you had," said my friend Larry, who's been through two of each. Since marriage and divorce are parallel institutions, it was no surprise when Judith Wallerstein's widely cited study of divorced couples revealed that joint custody worked best when a pattern of shared parenting had already been established. While divorce exposes buried assumptions about money and power, it invariably brings the truth about fatherhood out of the closet as well.

The film *Kramer vs. Kramer* arguably did more to wake men up to the deeper meaning of fatherhood than all those years of *Father Knows Best*—or as Roseanne Barr more accurately described family life in the fifties, "Father Knows Squat." The anthropological view that men have to be yoked tightly to women to become more sensitive may in fact be a slower, more draining route to higher evolution. It's men who are suddenly unyoked who can take nothing for granted again, including their children. Many fathers in those two-parent families who appear so admirably in

Whitehead's statistics might find that, should they suffer the rude shock of divorce, they are no more than gray-flannel ghosts to their kids.

For many brave men who run large corporations, fly super-sized jets, or construct huge skyscrapers, the prospect of a weekend alone with two small children can be terrifying. Those who survive the first quakes and continue, however, discover an intimacy they come to treasure. Some of the most moving personal stories in the *New York Times* "His" column were written by men who discovered fatherhood after divorce. They made "visitation" sound like something a married man might like to try.

If all those men in Washington who became enmeshed in the power dream of the Vietnam era had actually raised the kids whose names they put in the lottery, chances are they would have been much slower to the draw. The national outrage following Susan Smith's grievous crime was unanimous and unambiguous: Where was the outrage when fathers were slaughtering fifty-eight thousand of our young?

In addition to a deeper knowledge of fatherhood, single and divorced men also become more conscious of housework, although the recidivism into old habits and expectations can be swift when they remarry. One friend in a second marriage has taken some of the benefits of divorce with her— the self-respect, the sense of entitlement. She arranges periodic separations, leaving for a week or two to visit sisters and friends, allowing her husband to remember where the pot roasts come from, how the clothes get home from the cleaners. Each time she returns from these mini-separations, she greets an effusively joyful man. Imagine: a wife whose services are routinely appreciated.

The Republican wives of the freshman congressmen could perform a vital service for the whole country if they would adjourn to an island for a few months. We'd be *really* grateful if they took all the ATM cards and credit cards with them. They could have a wonderful time and their husbands would benefit immediately. Instead of drawing a blank during their deliberations, they might get a fuzzy picture of what those welfare mothers are doing all day.

Since most families today depend on two paychecks, a woman doesn't have to be single to resent the discounted wages we are paid, though it has more serious consequences if you are. Although most working women yearn for equal pay and a more mother-friendly work environment, the front liners pressing hardest for change are those who cannot quit. Doing double duty as the sole crumb-winners and primary caretakers, working mothers also have the daunting job of educating corporations about family values. We have no choice about becoming the most vocal "harpies" at work. It's no fun, these tedious, repetitive campaigns for equal pay, flexitime, day care, health benefits, and sick leave. We could use some help from the Christian Coalition here. Even if Ralph Reed can't be persuaded to be allies with divorced mothers, there are plenty of married women and a growing number of working fathers who would benefit greatly from a "pro-family" workplace.

Since the pro-family movement seems to be in the grip of the same fanatical need for order and conformity that saturated the fifties, they might consider advocating universal divorce instead of forced marriage. Even those lucky couples in great and happy unions might gain some insights into their relationship if they regularly reviewed the myriad, minute details behind their vows to love and honor. A good divorce is actually the reconstruction of a shaky marriage, and success depends on faithful adherence to tough new postmarital vows: You have to talk. Take nothing for granted. Keep negotiating the rest of your lives. Respect your history together. Honor commitments to your children. Divide everything equitably—bills, assets, time with the kids. Be fair . . . even when you'd rather shoot each other.

My former husband and I ruefully acknowledge that it took nearly two decades, and millions of words, to rebuild trust and friendship in our own postnuclear family. But we are hardly the only family out here in the frontier that has expanded rather than shrunk with divorce. "Your basic extended family today includes your ex-husband or -wife, your ex's new mate, your new mate, possibly your new mate's ex, and any new mate that your new mate's ex has acquired," Delia Ephron wrote in *Funny Sauce*. "It consists entirely of people who are not related by blood, many of whom can't stand each other." Just like traditional families everywhere.

If we could set the statistics aside for a moment and turn down the heat in the family-values debate, the lines between the irresponsible Them and the righteous Us begin to blur. Whether we are raising children within the institution of marriage or the institution of divorce, we need exactly the same things: self-respect, enlightened fathers, equitable wages, good schools, dependable support, a sturdy kinship network. It takes a whole village to raise a child, as the African proverb goes.

The main problem in debating with family-values evangelists is that they are uninterested in learning about anybody else's religion. The habit of either/or thinking—either you're a good nuclear family or you don't count as a family at all—prohibits recognition that some parts of marriage are bad and some parts of divorce are good. If divorce were *de*stigmatized, all families could experiment with structures that would better suit their personalities and situations. I know the virtues of diversity are hard for true believers in the nuclear family, but changing the family to fit the people is hardly a radical new idea.

Suffragist and civil-rights leader Crystal Eastman excited public discussion in 1923 with an essay called "Marriage Under Two Roofs," describing how she kept her marriage intact by moving herself and the children into a separate apartment. There was an immediate and dramatic improvement in family relationships after she eliminated her husband from the breakfast table. He was not a morning person, and reacted to children's early-rising energy about the same way plastic explosives respond to an electrical charge. I sent Eastman's essay to a friend who'd reached a crisis stage in her marriage and was stuck between the petals of I-love-him, I-love-him-not. She couldn't leave, couldn't stay, so she did a little of both.

She remained married but moved to another wing of the house. Four years later, her husband is regularly invited to spend the night with her—but sleeping together, like everything else, is a choice now rather than an unexamined habit and greatly depends on how affections have fared through the day. Though he'd hotly resisted the change when she first proposed it, defending his marital rights, he eventually understood that if he didn't at least try there could be no marriage at all. Now he prefers their new arrangement, having discovered that earned love is a lot more intimate and satisfying than love on demand.

This would no doubt come as a surprise to former Senator Jeremiah Denton, who had enormous difficulty understanding the concept of marital rape when it was first introduced to Congress fifteen years ago. Most of Senator Denton's information about women and families came from the Moral Majority. "Damn it," he said to the Senate Judiciary Committee, "when you get married, you kind of expect you're going to get a little sex." One way or another.

As one of the self-absorbed divorced mothers under assault, I can't think of a worse idea than to stigmatize single working mothers. How can it be in the best interests of children when a culture holds their mothers in contempt? Why quadruple the work of women raising children alone by undermining their dignity and credibility from every direction? Want a reason for the free-floating rage among the remorseless teenagers in poor neighborhoods who don't seem to care about other human beings? Start here: These kids have been taught to loathe their mothers from the day they were born.

Hardly anyone is more alarmed about urban violence and poverty than the mothers of children most vulnerable to them, but nowhere do the family-values preachers acknowledge that our hearts might be breaking, too, raising children in a society where they have to pass through metal detectors before they can study the multiplication tables, where it's easier and cheaper for a ten-year-old to buy a handgun than a pair of sneakers. Aiming howitzers of loaded facts at mothers, the family-values warriors have bravely taken on an enemy that poses about the same challenge as the terrified natives on the island of Grenada. The problem with using scapegoats—aside from the unsettling possibility of becoming one—is that the fever of prejudice delays the necessary action that still must be taken to solve the problems.

There is always a nod, among the more responsible experts studying the family, that there might be "other factors" besides women's selfishness for the alarming deterioration of family life: the overwhelming violence in movies and on television; domestic battery and sexual abuse; wage discrimination; the disappearance of jobs that can support a family; the redistribution of wealth that shifted 90 percent of all income to the top fifth of the population; the AIDS epidemic; the number of guns in the U.S. homes; and the disintegration of good public education. And never mentioned in the same paragraph with "the rising divorce rate" is this factor, directly responsible for the death of thousands of marriages: 3.5 million men in my generation were enlisted during the Vietnam era—more than 1.5 million in combat, spending critical years of their youth under fire in a jungle in one of the most violent and dehumanizing conflicts in history.

The youngest and poorest soldiers in any American war, the Vietnam veterans were reabsorbed into mostly urban families. For the past two decades, a continuing flood of stories about these veterans has revealed their persistent trouble reentering civilian life. These millions of physically and psychologically scarred men, *concentrated in one generation*, have sons coming of age today. Since the cyclical nature of domestic violence is so well documented by now, couldn't the scary, embattled, emotionally numb, and dangerously armed youths that so frighten us today be another terrible warning sign that the wars we wage will inevitably come home?

Before we restigmatize divorce, which would imperil women and children living with tragically damaged men, shouldn't we first raise at least one generation unburdened by the legacy of war? I long to hear a family-values politician argue passionately that until we stop sending young men, future fathers, into the unfixable ruin of modern war, there is no possibility of bringing psychologically healthy, nonviolent, civilized children into this world. These urgent social issues are not "other factors," just as the symptoms listed in fine print on the warning labels of powerful medications are not "side-effects." These are real-effects, these are *the* factors. Maybe that's why the pro-family leaders are so mad at divorced women—we have unleashed on society the intemperate behavior that former generations of wives were obliged to contain at home.

Incest and sexual abuse, for example, are among the other factors Whitehead lists for the rising divorce rate—

though lesser concerns than the central problem of women's "selfishness." According to her statistics, incest accounts for only a small percentage of divorces. That the majority don't file for that reason hardly reduces the horror for those that do—and sociologist Diana Russell has confirmed that the incidence of sexual abuse is far greater than this meager percentage represents. Either wives and mothers are disguising their motives under "no fault" to get out as fast as they can, or they are *not* divorcing when they should.

In a society where single mothers cannot support their families, a dependent woman with children cannot leave even when the safety of the children is the very reason she must. Faced with social ostracism and almost certain poverty, mothers trapped in abusive marriages are understandably frightened by the odds of independent survival. Maybe "power corrupts," but powerlessness corrupts as well. Increasing the sanctions against divorce would further endanger the mothers in this statistical minority even if most experts would undoubtedly protest, "Goodness, we didn't mean *you*—we only meant to punish those selfish women."

The restigmatization plan is a shame, of course. There's plenty of suffering without manufacturing pointless misery, and it's not likely to bring many pioneers in from the frontiers. It's a hard life, but you don't need vodka in your grapefruit most mornings. For one thing, there's too damn much to do every day. But the main attraction is that women don't have to shut up out here. Talk, in fact, is crucial to life in the postnuclear world.

Family secrets still make it impossible to know all the stories behind the divorce rate. Suppose we suspended judgment for a decade, called a truce in this domestic Cold War between Us and Them. In the present culture, where incest and domestic violence are still too tragically real, where the majority of families can no longer survive on a single paycheck, we cannot all live the same way. History proves we never did. We never will. Forcing all couples into one family structure assumes we are the same, and we are not. Some of us are gay, some are straight; some of us are gifted with young children, some are inept with them; some of us thrive on affection, some don't know how to show it; some of us are dangerous, some are afraid; some of us are morning people, and some of us shouldn't risk human contact before noon. Some of us can live with vodka in the grapefruit and some of us can't. It's absurdly cruel to force this diverse population into a painfully narrow family that is, quite literally, killing us. A truly kinder, gentler nation would expand the institution of the family, making room for all God's people.

Democracy can't thrive without tolerance, and tolerance requires constant practice. Our families, for all their imperfections, are the classrooms for those lessons. A long-time friend whose pioneering family now includes her ex-husband, his gay lover, her two daughters and their boyfriends, her own significant other, and several children-in-laws, invited them all to her youngest son's college graduation last summer. Also attending the reunion was her eighty-four-year-old widowed mother, a devout Christian who'd been deeply shaken when her much-loved minister son-in-law came out ten years ago and initiated this family evolution. Worried that her mother had been disturbed by the obvious affections flowing freely in all directions, she asked her on the drive home if anything had made her uneasy. She found out that yes, there was one thing her mother found disturbing. She thought her former son-in-law was "a little underdressed for the graduation," she said. "His shirt was nice, but I wished he'd worn a tie."

A tie. My friend laughed and wept when she told me this story, her face beaming with the bewildered joy of a woman who'd witnessed a miracle. The family-values evangelists who are so sure God wants the Americans they know to live in nuclear families are probably right . . . and so is my friend's faith in her holy family. According to Christian doctrine, God has crafted a rather unusual existence for Himself, living without a wife in a creative trinity with two other males, one of which is a bird. This is exactly the familial arrangement so many fundamentalists find deeply disturbing in San Francisco and New York. God not only elevated a single woman who found herself implausibly pregnant to Queen of Heaven but accepted His son's life in a same-sex commune with a dozen apostles. If we all just behaved like this Christian God, tolerance could replace righteousness as the national virtue.

VIII

A Talking Cure for the Silent Majority

ON THE STREETS of downtown Petoskey in the summer, throngs of color-coordinated, good-natured parents ushered almost iridescently healthy children in and out of restaurants and shops near the McLean and Eakin bookstore, my main hangout on Main Street. Coming from my New York neighborhood, I felt like I'd been dropped on the set of a Frank Capra movie: angels were watching over these people, and grace came with a lot of money. The dream of the Christian, pro-family movement seemed almost idyllically realized here. This exterior happiness invited cynicism that it wasn't real, or couldn't be maintained without hypocrisy or repression. Where do people who like pornography go for a good time around here? To outsiders, this community would appear to be playing the national game of "Let's Pretend" to the extreme.

All the headlines in the news were being lived by the local residents here, you'd learn over coffee at Shirley's, but walking down Main Street they weren't in-your-face. Since

AIDS, mental illness, domestic violence, and divorce observe no geographical or class boundaries, midwestern families have to wrestle with their percentage of human grief and tragedy, as well as the psychological reverberations these shocks set in motion. Here, too, there are worries about the violent Norms, the Limbaugh dittoheads, the wives who begin their days with spiked grapefruit. There is still plenty of poverty and hunger in wealthy Northern Michigan, in trailer park encampments just outside Petoskey, largely invisible from the road. These realities would be hashed over during counter deliberations at the Americana every morning, but even the alarmist canaries here seemed to be in better psychological shape, more optimistic and hopeful about the future. Why?

Perhaps it's easier to see the big picture in a small town, but the people I met here still think like my dad: When trouble comes, get in it together. Grassroots activism is not something that makes it into the news very often, moving inch by unspectacular inch, and you'd need a time-lapse camera to catch it on film. Local issues were generally introduced around people's kitchen tables first, evolving slowly through reading groups, city council hearings, church organizations, and coffee klatches until the heartland urge to do something was sufficiently pumped up. Then the massive fund-raising and volunteering began, in the barn-raising spirit of the past, which eventually produced these clean streets and healthy children. A body politic of perpetrators, rescuers, victims, and bystanders were all bound together here, talking or arguing with each other as if their lives depended on it. One talk led to another.

Eighteen years ago, Jan Mancinelli took a $9,000 job with the Women's Resource Center of Northern Michigan, funded by a CETA grant, and worked with a cadre of volunteers to do something about the problem of domestic violence. The Center rented a small house and opened a shelter which, like others across the country, filled to capacity almost immediately. Years of continuous fund-raising and grant writing kept the shelter going. A resale shop run by volunteers eventually produced enough profits to make a down payment on a more spacious facility.

The degrees of separation between the Center's activist, middle-class housewives and their black-and-blue clients were not so great, apparently, that they forgot how important a good night's sleep was to a woman trying to get her life back on track. Maybe they'd discussed what kind of environment they would need, or had needed once, over drinks—I would guess it took quite a few rounds—because the next property the Center acquired was a large Victorian mansion on the outskirts of town, with a contemplative garden and wood-burning stoves, beveled glass windows and beautiful oak floors. In addition to shelter and safety, clients received guidance from staff counselors. The Center opened daycare and preschool programs to the community and provided job training and employment counseling to displaced homemakers. The thriving, well-managed Center eventually attracted contributions from some of the wealthy summer residents, but the bulk of its support came from small, regular donations from its year-round neighbors.

How did Jan keep from sounding strident and hysterical when she brought her unending lists from the shelter to the responsible parties in the community? "I go sailing in my little boat every chance I get," she said, laughing. She's even gone AWOL from the director's office when the wind was just right, though rarely for long. Once you get clear of the mess on the shore and start thinking about what human beings really need, it doesn't seem outrageous that we should find common ground and claim it. Now administering a budget of more than a million dollars a year, making every penny count, "Jan could be the CEO of General Motors," her friends said fondly.

When Beltway insiders venture out here and observe

this folk society in operation, the exterior equanimity is mistaken for innocence about the Other America, the class war, the racism tearing our country apart. The greater civility in these communities is rarely perceived as the result of deep thinking and hard work, even to leaders of social movements. A "midwestern radical" is still an oxymoron— despite all the wobblies and feminists and farmers who have been raising public consciousness from here. It annoys the hell out of the natives when the Big Thinks arrive from the coasts and talk to them like they've never heard of social-justice movements. But that's the BTs' problem.

"Sometimes I fancy that we now pay therapists the way an earlier generation bought brushes or Bibles or pep tonic from traveling salesmen," Joan Frank writes. "We are hungry for the contact; for purpose, faith and possibility." We long to be shaken, because "no matter how often our teeth vibrate after reading the tragic headline or even after dodging our own terrifying close call, we soon slide back into numbness and to a strange water level of discontent," she said. She believes "that you can remember possibility, that you can make yourself see and feel with something like the hair-raising X-ray vision of childhood but that you have to work at it in odd ways to get back even a shiver."

Political depression is a kind of soul-grief, the personal toll exacted from caring people who live in a society where "people first" is merely a slogan. The only cure is to keep talking until all of Us and Them recognize that the body politic is a We, a kind of social ecosystem in which every part depends on the health and survival of the other. The bystander blues that are sweeping the country could be a healthy sign that consciousness is stretching again, though it's always painful when innocence ruptures. To grow into knowledgeable bystanders, of course, innocence has to go.

We're going to need a new kind of therapy to see us

through the difficult transition from innocent bystander to knowledgeable bystander. "The old idea of self-caused (endogenic) depression" simply doesn't apply to sufferers of political unreality, psychiatrist James Hillman and columnist Michael Ventura reaffirm in *We've Had a Hundred Years of Psychotherapy and the World's Getting Worse*. Hillman criticizes modern therapy, deeply invested in the pleasure principle and focused almost exclusively on the self, for teaching disturbed citizens to cope and not protest, to adapt and not rebel—essentially, "to normalize their oddity." By encouraging the politically depressed to "work within your situation" rather than "refuse the unacceptable," Hillman writes, "therapy is collaborating with what the state wants: docile plebes."

When Nobel laureate Heinrich Böll was asked what he thought the most dangerous flaw in the character of the German people was, the great novelist answered in a word: "Obedience." We Americans, proudly rooted in a heritage of rugged individualism, do not generally think of ourselves as obedient—and yet, as Dr. Frankl observed, we have followed orders again and again to "be happy." If the personal joy we obediently pursued for the past fifty years had turned out to be a solid instead of a liquid—grounded in meaning, attached to feelings—the body politic would probably not be having the vapors today. Since so many of us are having trouble being happy without reason, treatment for our national depression has to start by recovering our senses.

When there is as much suffering as our newspapers hold today, the daily witnesses are strongly tempted to detach from their feelings. "Indifference, which on its own does no apparent or immediate positive harm, ends by washing itself in the very horrors it means to have nothing to do with. Hoping to confer no hurt, indifference finally grows lethal," Cynthia Ozick wrote. When bystanders witness political events without thinking, without feeling, "indifference shuts down the humane, and does it deliberately," Ozick said. "Indifference is as determined—and as forcefully muscular—as any blow."

The danger of this anesthetized state is that consent for preposterous ideas can be squeezed out of us. When pollsters catch us in this state of cultivated indifference, exhausted by suffering, our leaders can easily read our answers to mean, "Do what you want, we don't care." But by putting the severed parts of the personal and political self back together—"making it whole," as Virginia Woolf advised—bystanders can emerge from the zombified state of "docile plebe" and start coming to.

Minds defrosting after forty years of Cold War thinking will no doubt ache, confronted with the unreality all around us. In a culture deeply embedded in mendacity, being simply human—alive to our thoughts and our feelings—is an act of tremendous will. There is so much untruth in our language, putting the meaning back into our lives means thinking and double thinking and rethinking. It will be necessary to question every tradition, every loyalty that has passed for normal in the past.

Had we been paying closer attention to the subtext of sound-bites, for example, we might have registered an objection to former President Bush's comment after Anita Hill's dramatic opening testimony, when reporters caught him in his shirtsleeves on the White House lawn and asked for his reaction.

"I didn't even watch it," he replied, almost contemptuous of the question. He didn't have to, he said, because nothing could alter his support for Clarence Thomas.

At the time, we knew this comment was supposed to inspire us to think, "What a loyal guy, standing by his man through 'this whole ugly thing,'" as he called it. Had all of our cylinders been firing—had we been thinking about the future and remembering feelings of the past—we might have thought instead, "Wait a minute . . . here we are glued to our TV sets, and the guy who appointed Clarence Thomas didn't even *watch?*" Women in the audience might have heard this message: "It doesn't matter if you lie or tell the truth. Make trouble for my man, I won't even listen."

Bush apparently didn't know, "the whole ugly thing" involved an estimated 85 percent of all American women—and neither, for a moment, did we. In October 1991, 37 percent of bystanders polled "believed Clarence Thomas" while 27 percent "believed Anita Hill." A year later, *Newsweek* polled us again and reported in December 1992 that 51 percent now thought Anita Hill was telling the truth while only 34 percent believed Clarence Thomas. Did we lie in the first poll? Or were we, as I suspect, temporarily out of touch with our own reality?

When the pollsters called the first time, we repeated the facts and opinions we'd absorbed from the media. What happened in the next year that eventually caused us to reject the facts and opinions manufactured by public relations? We talked. We broke into the "chasm of speechlessness" where we kept our secrets. More facts, long buried, emerged. A few months after the cacophony of the confirmation hearings were over, my friend Libby's retired parents called from Florida and quietly apologized for an incident that had happened some twenty years earlier, when their daughter was twelve.

They'd been thinking things over and were sorry, now, about how they'd responded when she complained about the "nasty passes" from a boy down the street. They hadn't thought of it as "sexual harassment" then—nobody did. They had coached her to manage the situation a little less emotionally—to adjust, adapt, change her route home from school. Now, they said, they wished they had dealt with the problem "out there." Libby shivered when she told this story. It came involuntarily when she remembered the boy, the twenty years, her parents' genuine regret.

Anita Hill's testimony provoked millions of such shivers in the body politic. In that intervening year between calls from the pollsters, we'd listened to—maybe cried over—the personal stories of dozens of friends. Hearts engaged, we registered a major bounce on the public cardiogram in *Newsweek*. Had we known these stories just one year earlier, Clarence Thomas might not be sitting on the Supreme Court today. A political nomination can't survive in a culture which won't support it, however strong a president's endorsement. Zoë Baird lost her confirmation because "the public reacted strongly"—and quickly, perhaps because far fewer of us were implicated in Baird's ethical lapse than in the omnipresent crime of sexual harassment.

"Before a secret is told one can often feel the weight of it in the atmosphere," Susan Griffin wrote. "I am beginning to believe that we know everything, that all history, including the history of each family, is part of us . . . when we hear any secret revealed, a secret about a grandfather, or an uncle, or a secret about the battle of Dresden in 1945, our lives are made suddenly clearer to us, as the unnatural heaviness of unspoken truth is dispersed. For perhaps we are like stones; our own history and the history of the world embedded in us, we hold a sorrow deep within and cannot weep until that history is sung." So what stops us from talking, from coming to in time to prevent history from repeating itself?

Getting yanked out of a virtual reality in which you're the hero into an actual life where you share some responsibility is a huge psychological undertaking. Many of the nuclear physicists involved in the arms race, facing the results of their labor, eventually became the most ardent activists against nuclear weapons. But retired Brigadier General Paul Tibbets, the pilot who flew the *Enola Gay* and dropped the first bomb in human history, was deeply offended when the Smithsonian planned an exhibit on the fiftieth anniversary of that historic occasion that put all the parts together.

This before-and-after view of our history "would have linked the unlinkable: the burnished plane with the human suffering it caused and continues to cause; smiling shots of boisterous young airmen with unbearable images of seared victims; the consciousness of those who fought in World War II with the consciousness of those who grew up in the penumbra of World War III; the celebratory with the crematory; the just with the unjust; victory with defeat," wrote Tom Engelhardt, author of *The End of Victory Culture.* Would it be hard for patriotic Americans to see this whole, complicated view of history? Very hard . . . especially because the exhibit was canceled before it ever opened last year. The Smithsonian historians had drawn immense criticism not only from General Tibbets, who called the truths they assembled "a package of insults," but from the media, Congress, and veterans' organizations.

The bystanders who resolve to know the meaning of cultural events face multiple problems, beginning with our own internal resistance and unacknowledged guilt. Why is it so important to know? Because whatever the big picture, the movie can't play without us. The atrocities of World War II could never have been carried out unless decent citizens in Germany agreed not to "know" what was going on. Mass denial was achieved only partly through propaganda— the "transportation" of 6 million Jews also depended on a fragmented workforce, comfortably distanced from the consequences of individual actions. Ignorant of the whole picture, a French bureaucrat could therefore follow orders from afar and issue this memo to his own police: "The German authorities have set aside especially for that purpose enough trains to transport 30,000 Jews. It is therefore necessary that the arrests made should correspond to the schedule of the train." Even the German SS troops who made most of the arrests were separated from the actual murders—that was done by "gas ovens," operated by the prisoners themselves. "These crimes, these murders of millions, were all carried out in absentia, as if by no one in particular," Griffin observed.

As my friend Patricia O'Toole wrote in a letter from the Wilson Library in Chapel Hill last year, after holding in her hand a bill of sale from a slave auction for thirty human beings, "the all-in-a-day's-work quality of it is heart-stopping." But hearts immersed in the virtual realities of fascism or slavery didn't stop—though some may have skipped a few beats—because eradicating Jews and purchasing Africans had become "normal" behavior in the culture supporting them. And hearts immersed in the Kinder, Gentler Nation no longer stop when Eddie the Loop, or any of the homeless windshield washers working the exit ramps, asks for a quarter. We've learned to look away.

Philosopher and social reformer Bertrand Russell once declared that, in case he met God, he would say to him, "Sir, you did not give us enough information." Kurt Vonnegut said he would add to that, "All the same, Sir, I'm not persuaded that we did the best we could with the information we had. Toward the end there, anyway, we had tons of information." We "knew," even before the specific details of ruined world economies and toxic wastes were revealed, as more KGB files and CIA papers make headlines around the world.

How did we know? At the military hospital in Oak Ridge, Tennessee, crazed patients who cried out during nightmares were "disappeared" into isolation wards. Nurses on the night shift still talked in whispers, months and years later, about what they heard. Karen Silkwood is killed in a car accident and the briefcase of papers she had promised an investigative reporter cannot be found. Nobody thinks she could have just forgotten to bring them. If the full details of the Iran-contra affair are ever disclosed, if the Nixon tapes are ever released from legal blockades at the National Archives, if the gag orders in the settlement of critical medical suits are ever lifted, we will not be surprised by the devastating secrets they contain. We already know and feel them—they show up in our cynicism about politics, our crime-ridden streets, our arrhythmic polls. For the bystanders not only consent to the culture—we live in it.

Certainly, future historians studying the photos and news stories about the arms race, global pollution, our immune-system dysfunctions, and the whopping world debt amassed by the Superpowers will think it odd we didn't "know" what was going on. Before any radioactive wastes can be dumped in our deserts and oceans, they must first pass through millions of minds: Secret plans have to be discussed, secret orders have to be issued, secret papers have to be typed, secret cargo has to be transported, secret destinations have to be reached. All this work must be done by people without anyone wondering, anywhere along the long route to the North Pole, "Say, what's *in* this stuff?"

As Professor Bellah and his colleagues point out in *The Good Society*, the homeless were not dropped on our streets *deus ex machina*—they arrived through human actions and social choices: "The market-driven conversion of single-room-occupancy hotels into upscale tourist accommodations, government urban renewal projects that revitalized downtowns while driving up rents and reducing housing for the poor, economic changes that eliminated unskilled jobs paying enough to support a family, the states' 'deinstitutionalization' of the mentally ill and reduced funding of local community health programs."

Each of these "systems" responsible for the despair

today are comprised of individual people. The homeless, the camp inmates of our cities, had to pass unnoticed through the thoughts of real estate brokers, economists, CEOs, human-resource personnel, mental-health experts, state legislators, county judges, voters and taxpayers, my friends, your friends, you and me, while none of us "knew" what we were doing.

However painful or compromising it may be to unveil our secrets, clinging to our innocence ultimately offers no protection. The truth about how we govern and do business eventually leaks out everywhere. We eat it in our food, breathe it in our air, step over it on the streets, observe it in our paychecks, see it in our X-rays, feel it in our bones. Being an innocent bystander in today's world requires blotting out so much reality that, finally, it takes more effort to avoid the truth than to own it.

"Therapy is going to have to go out the door with the client, maybe even make home visits, or at least walk down the street," Hillman concludes. The American Association of Marriage and Family Therapy is increasingly aware that political structures are directly responsible for much of the pathology we are experiencing today. In *Women and Power*, family therapist Thelma Jean Goodrich redefines the goal of therapy as helping a client "gain whatever resources are necessary to remove oneself from a condition of oppression." Goodrich says that "a social order that studies war, rewards competitiveness, restricts resources, promotes isolation and punishes those who are colored, female or poor" requires therapists today to "stop using our sessions to fix up the people so the system works better and start fixing up the systems so the people work better." She questions the efficacy of helping clients in therapy without also engaging in social activism.

If our therapists were to accept the invitation to get out of the office and walk out the door with clients, what would such activist counseling encourage us to do? Certainly, before recommending any kind of "responsible action," it would first be necessary to identify the powers and limitations of our four social roles in the body politic—perpetrator, victim, rescuer, or bystander. Since most of us are acutely aware that we are not Henry Kissinger or Donald Trump, the influence of the bystander appears minuscule. We do not have the cultural clout of the Joint Chiefs, who can stop an executive order merely by calling a meeting and arranging their hands and lips just so. Nor are we as invisible and anonymous as Eddie the Loop or baby Christopher's young mother, who might not even know what executive orders can do. We have only the power of public opinion that, as it stands, is being preframed in the polls.

If the body politic is to start bouncing back to life in the polls, two essential psychological tasks face the bystanders: to know, that is, reconnect meaning to what we are witnessing; and to feel, to actively resist indifference. Essentially, Ozick suggests that when bad times deliver us to "a place where there are no human beings, *be* one." The recovery movement has spent ten years hosting meetings where people reconnect with the lost parts of themselves. Activist therapy would proceed to the next step, grafting these healing cells back onto the body politic.

As zombified bystanders come back to life, they would be encouraged to use the power of knowing "out loud," as it were. It was knowing and feeling that led the Danish bystanders fifty years ago to put the Star of David on their sleeves, offering protection and solidarity for Jewish neighbors. It was fear of this same populist knowing a few years ago that brought back the first 100 of the 400 Palestinians deported by the Israelis, with promises for the rest. Fear that Americans would bounce in their support caused one Israeli official to remark how much harder it was to conduct cleansings with "everyone watching on CNN." Exactly.

It was not the threat of U.S. bombs that brought about

the reversal in Israeli policy—it was the power of collective thought. And it wasn't just watching—it was knowing what we saw. When the Palestinians were returned, we felt the momentary exhilaration in the power of our role, telling world leaders for a change, "This will not stand." But even one "knowing" bystander in a culture of denial can make an enormous difference.

Responding to the absurdities of current politics, Gregory Daniels, a reader in Beverly Hills, remembered a lesson from an Introduction to Psychology class years ago: "In this experiment, a room full of people all agree that a two-foot rod is longer than a three-foot rod, and the one person who isn't in on it will most often deny the evidence of his eyes and agree with them. But if there's one other person in the room who agrees with the test subject, then the subject will almost never give in to the group's wrong opinions." Both perpetrators and rescuers are dependent on the power of the witness—it is the bystander who nods agreement or looks away when an unwelcome truth is aired.

Everyone won't be happy if we start finding relief for political depressions by knowing out loud. If we refuse to consent to certain absurdities that powerful perpetrators are most fond of—trickle-down economics, let's say—the usual names are likely to be hauled out: strident and hysterical, antipatriotic, godless humanists, special-interest groups, bleeding hearts, and whistle blowers—usually uttered with contempt, designed to make us feel selfish or crazy. In his best-selling book, Rush Limbaugh identifies people whose hearts ache over political suffering as "liberal compassion fascists," and anyone who supports the green movement is "a long-haired maggot-infested FM-type environmentalist wacko." These names are hard on bystanders who shy away from conflict.

In 1962, when Rachel Carson published *Silent Spring*, her prophetic book about the long-term damage putting toxic pesticides and carcinogens into our fields and streams would do to our food supply, *Time* magazine accused her of "frightening and arousing" readers. One leading scientist dismissed her worries about future generations as insincere because she was "a spinster who had no children." History provides a different view than her contemporaries: thirty-one years later, the *New Yorker* would report that "women with the highest exposure to DDT have a risk of developing breast cancer four times as great as that of women with the least exposure."

And if the whole story of the Vietnam era is ever told, history may have a different view of the much derided anti-war movement. "I still think a fair amount about the 60s and trying to be a good hippie," Mark Vonnegut, now a pediatrician and father in Massachusetts wrote in an afterward to his memoir, *The Eden Express*. "We were not the spaced-out, flaky, self-absorbed, wimpy, whiny flower children in movies and TV shows alleging to depict the times. It's true that we were too young, too inexperienced, and in the end too vulnerable to bad advice from middle-aged sociopathic gurus. Things eventually went bad, drugs took their toll, but before they went bad, hippies did a lot of good. Brave, honest, and true, and they paid a price. I'm sure no one will ever study it, but my guess is that there are as many disabled and deeply scarred ex-hippies as there are Vietnam vets. When all is said and done, the times were out of joint. Adults as much as said that they didn't have a clue what should be done and that it was up to us, the best, bravest, brightest children ever, to fix things up. We gave it our best shot, and I'm glad I was there."

Although most historical accounts of Anna O.'s hysterical depression end when she severs her relationship with Freud and his associates, her life did not end there. Under her own name, Bertha Pappenheim, she became a prominent social worker, intellectual, and organizer. Judith Herman recounts that "in the course of a long and fruitful career she directed an orphanage for girls, founded a feminist organization for Jewish women, and traveled throughout Europe and the Middle East to campaign against the sexual exploitation of women and children. In the words of a colleague, 'A volcano lived in this woman . . . her fight against the abuse of women and children was almost a physically felt pain for her.'" Bertha Pappenheim chose not to detach from the pain of her childhood—she let it move her. Then she moved the world.

It's going to be tough for those of us conditioned to the quick fix, acclimated to the role of bystander, to become talkers in our communities, seers in our corporations. But if enough of us suffering political depressions become activist bystanders, committed to knowing out loud, there would eventually be just too many of us to ignore. "Change takes time," the cultural adage warns, but it is really resistance that takes time. The fear of being ousted from the herd, of finding ourselves in the margins of public approval, prevents the silent majority from saying what we know. It might help to imagine, before answering any more polls, "What would I say if I knew I had only thrity days left to live?"

Since there are myriad personal and professional difficulties to face if we are to start "knowing out loud," activist therapy would do well to provide weekly support groups for bystanders recovering from the blues. James Hillman suggests such a network is already in place, in the half-million recovery groups that meet weekly. "During Franklin D. Roosevelt's presidency, recovery meant dealing with one-third of a nation, which he said were ill fed, ill clothed, and ill housed. He invented the NRA, the National Recovery Act. With a little spin and a little shove, all the 500,000 recovery meetings going on each week all across the U.S.A. could turn from individualism to the body politic, recovering some of the political concern for the plight of the nation that necessitated recovery groups in the first place. As I see it, we cannot recover alone or even in support groups. We need communal recovery, recovery of communal feeling, and each group provides the nucleus of that feeling."

The leaders of the Fort Wayne Feminists, when our nerves were frayed and the sisterhood was about to self-destruct once more, would mandate a Lock-In. We'd all get into our cars and drive to the YWCA retreat at Dallas Lake, set up our sleeping bags in the bunks of the Big House, start the water boiling in the kitchen, and lock the doors. We began talking, and nobody left until we finished, said the hard words that needed to be said so we could come back to reality again. We were astounded when news anchors reported from Iceland that Reagan and Gorbachev were meeting "for two hours today," as if that were a lot of time. Shit, two hours. These men were talking about *global* peace, and it took the sisters four days just to unravel the mess in our tiny slice of the country. In two hours, we'd barely finished passing the family pictures around. If the meetings had been planned in Fort Wayne, those boys would have been locked up.

The talking cure is hardly a "quick fix," of course—the dependence on quick fixes is part of our political pathology. One of the most prevalent lies during election campaigns is that it's possible to change forty years of Cold War thinking in the "first hundred days" or "first three months" of a new administration. If it takes two teams of therapists and lawyers a year or more to usher one warring couple who once loved each other to a common understanding of money, property, child care, college tuitions, and alimony—as well as who might owe recognition or apologies to whom—it is impossible to believe one president can lead 250 million people thrown together willy-nilly into a mutually satisfactory settlement on the national budget, health care, child-support programs, mass transportation, religious practices, educational institutions, defense strategies, crime prevention—not to mention who has been taking advantage of whom for how long. Certainly, a national family of this size, wrestling with issues this huge, will need at least the "first hundred days" just to learn how to pronounce everybody's name. To achieve a genuine metanoia in national consciousness—for we cannot change behavior without first changing the way we think—would probably take the better part of the next one hundred years. Even then, we could not relax.

Genuine change from the inside out takes much longer, but has the advantage of being more permanent. It took the women's movement more than two decades to effect change through "small talk." In typical grassroots fashion, it started with trusted friends in consciousness-raising groups, where women mustered the courage to tell the truth about their lives. At first, these groups of talking heads were lightly dismissed in the media—if they were noticed at all—as a few whiners and complainers. Ten years later, marches and demonstrations drew millions of supporters. Without guns, without bloodshed, the bystanders in the women's movement accomplished a major social revolution without a single armed conflict. They marched, they rallied, but mostly they talked, firing words to initiate the most significant economic, social, and political revolution of the twentieth century.

One distinct advantage of using "small talk" as a weapon for social change is that it doesn't require any elaborate arms distribution or huge amounts of money. Everyone has a mouth, and everyone knows a secret. It doesn't require an elite corps of inside loyalists—the more people who start "knowing out loud," the better. Revolution by word of mouth is slow going, because it is working on two fronts simultaneously: While bystanders can change a culture by speaking up, the act of speaking up also changes the bystanders.

Reloading the Rabbit at the end of the summer, I missed Estaban but managed to get the Blue Box back in the trunk. I had turned in my assignment, two months late and four times over length again, but I wasn't quite through with these facts yet. "All things are true, but only partly true," as Frank had said. Once certain facts have scored the brain, they won't go away until you change them. The pursuit of meaning, like the pursuit of pleasure, is never over. I used to think that after so many "learning experiences," there would come a day you could quit thinking and striving and just be learned. I now believe this won't happen until I'm dead.

Composer Marvin Hamlisch was stopped short by this realization a few years ago when he came home to an empty house after winning several Oscars and was struck by the next thing he had to do: the cat litter needed changing. When Joan Frank told this story to a friend from abroad, he said, "Why do Americans always imagine it should ever be any other way? We all have to face the same mundaneness, the same terrors. We're all born alone, we're all going to die alone someday. It is the cat litter which is transcendent, not the Oscars!" He reminded her of the Zen adage "Before satori, chop wood and carry water; after satori, chop wood and carry water."

I still had the Blue Box to lug around with me, but I had some other realities now to think about on the way home. I thought about the views in upper Michigan, where residents didn't seem to need a brain tumor to get the big picture. A beautiful horizon seemed to do. It hadn't been Capraland where I went to recover—it was more like Lake Wobegon. The women were strong, even among the Norms and the dittoheads.

Julie Norcross, the energetic owner of McLean and Eakin's, said she'd chosen her grandmother's maiden name and her mother-in-law's maiden name to launch her first business. Her own mother, Gert Maus, was a grassroots businesswoman who with her husband Bill established a retail clothing chain from Northern Michigan to South Florida, one store and one state at a time, supporting five kids and innumerable employees who needed housing and education along the way. Now some twenty years into an active, philanthropic retirement, she was a regular guest at her daughter's dinner parties. Inspecting a rack of lamb between jokes about how kitchen utensils might subdue the Michigan Militia, Gert and her daughter were a two-woman mob of determination: This *will* be done. "You're going to love Mother," Julie had said. "She's a *riot*." And you would.

During a discussion one night about the appalling class division in America today, Gert wasn't buying all the blame heaped on the sluggish economy, an oblivious media, even our dissembling politicians, although she had some choice words for them. When her son-in-law Bill asked what she thought the problem was, Gert's fist came down on the table and rattled the silver as she said in a word: "Capitalism!" A successful capitalist herself, she didn't like the behavior among her own peers. Investors demanded too much money, too fast, from communities they drained and then left. She was disgusted by an economic policy that turned us into a looter nation, here and abroad, and as she talked you got a picture of how a few grandmothers on the Federal Reserve Board might help a lot. When Gert spoke, people listened. Here's to another grassroots movement, I prayed, while everyone else said grace that night: Dear God, thanks for the food and all, but please, what we desperately need are more Socially Responsible Investors.

With a great mother, great husband, great kids and

great friends, the *joie de vivre* at Julie's dinner table was contagious. A burned-out canary could be seated across from Gert's octogenarian friend Hattie, who'd driven 250 miles to their reunion in a red convertible, and soon be revived by her energy. And Julie was right when she told me "You're going to *love* Father Bill"—a Catholic priest who spontaneously delivered a stirring Sermon on the Mount when the discussion bogged down over minimum wage. You wouldn't think it possible, but you would stand behind the other guests in the hall when he gave his blessing at the end of the night, on the off chance some of this grace could spill over on you.

In the months after my coma, I had discovered peace was entirely comprehensible when it is grounded in meaning: It is not the goal but the result of thinking and striving. The route to peace is no twelve-stepper, the instruction manual not a how-to-get-it but a here's-why-you-have-it. It can't be gotten, say, by arguing for a few hours in Iceland and then strong-arming enemies into signing a treaty. If we were serious about peace, we would forget about it altogether and start concentrating on world understanding. It will take more than a few hours between naps to achieve a more thoughtful reality, the only environment peace can inhabit. Then it will come.

In those years after my close brush with death, I spent a lot of time thinking about "What if this had been *it?*" I remembered that lesson on the long drive home. The sorriest parts of my life were not the things I had done badly or clumsily, sometimes hurting innocent bystanders. I most regretted the things I hadn't done because I lacked sufficient nerve to risk disapproval from people who were important to me. Once I knew that we are all forgiven in the end for being who we are, doing what we must do, I became something of a dangerous woman. It's much easier to question all authorities when you don't need their approval.

While it was still as difficult as ever to break through the fuzz, get to the meaning, I no longer had to worry about whether I should. You Ask, you Tell.

I expect there will be unpleasantries, of course, when the long view of the horizon disappears and I'm stuck with the litter in the Blue Box again. A grassroots movement of disorganized bystanders is going to be a painfully slow revolution for people who take politics personally. The possibility of realizing all the changes we long for within our own lifetimes is remote. When the novelist Colette heard this complaint in a letter from her daughter, she wrote back, "Who said you should be happy? Do your work."

Had Colette not been in such a hurry, she might have added, "Remember: You cannot pursue happiness. But if you pursue meaning in your work, in your life, then happiness ensues."